# ANXIOUS
*for*
# NOTHING

MACARTHUR STUDY SERIES

*Alone with God*
*Divine Design*
*The Power of Suffering*
*Saved Without a Doubt*
*Standing Strong*

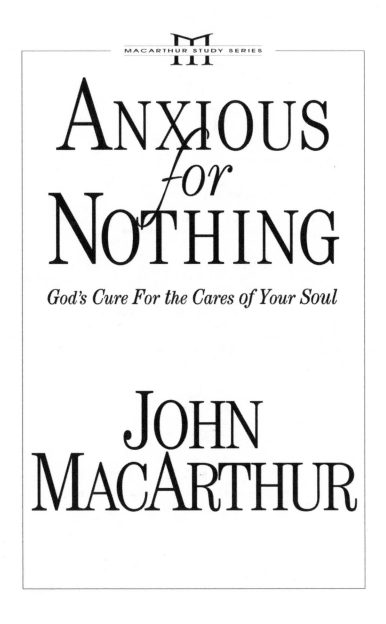

MACARTHUR STUDY SERIES

# ANXIOUS for NOTHING

*God's Cure For the Cares of Your Soul*

# JOHN MACARTHUR

David C Cook®

*transforming lives together*

ANXIOUS FOR NOTHING
Published by David C. Cook
4050 Lee Vance View
Colorado Springs, CO 80918 U.S.A.

David C. Cook Distribution Canada
55 Woodslee Avenue, Paris, Ontario, Canada N3L 3E5

David C. Cook U.K., Kingsway Communications
Eastbourne, East Sussex BN23 6NT, England

David C. Cook and the graphic circle C logo
are registered trademarks of Cook Communications Ministries.

Unless otherwise noted, Scripture references are from the *New American Standard Bible*,
© copyright 1960, 1971, 1995 by The Lockman Foundation. Used by permission.
Scripture quotations marked NIV are taken from the *Holy Bible, New International
Version®. NIV®.* Copyright © 1973, 1978, 1984 by International Bible Society. Used
by permission of Zondervan. All rights reserved; quotations marked KJV are from the
King James Version of the Bible. (Public Domain); quotations marked SCO are taken
from the New Scofield Reference Bible, King James Version, © 1967 by Oxford
University Press, Inc. Reprinted by permission; and quotations marked TLB are taken
from *The Living Bible*, © 1971, Tyndale House Publishers, Wheaton, IL 60189. Used
by permission. Italics in Scripture have been added by the author for emphasis.

Library of Congress Cataloging-in-Publication Data
MacArthur, John, 1939-
Anxious for nothing : God's cure for the cares of your soul / John MacArthur, Jr.-- 2nd
ed.
p. cm. -- (The MacArthur study series)
Rev. ed. of: Anxiety attacked.
Includes bibliographical references and indexes.
ISBN: 978-0-7814-4338-8
1. Anxiety--Biblical teaching. 2. Anxiety--Religious aspects--Christianity. 3. Bible--
Criticism, interpretation, etc. I. MacArthur, John, 1939- Anxiety attacked. II. Title.
BS680.A58M33 2006
248.8'6--dc22
2005033854

© 1993, 2006 by John MacArthur
Published under the title *Anxiety Attacked* by Victor Books, an imprint of Cook
Communications Ministries, in 1993. Original ISBN: 1-56476-128-2

Cover Design: Two Moore Designs/Ray Moore
Cover Photo Credit: PhotoSpin

Printed in the United States of America
Second Edition 2006

7 8 9 10 11 12 13 14

072508

# CONTENTS

# ACKNOWLEDGMENTS

Thanks to the staff of Grace to You who lent their editorial expertise to this project. Particular thanks to Allacin Morimizu, who arranged and edited this book from sermon transcripts.

# INTRODUCTION

*A*nxiety, *fear, worry,* and *stress* are familiar words in our day and familiar experiences to many. More and more we're hearing of an extreme form of anxiety referred to as a "panic attack." Some time ago, I observed one close at hand in the emergency room on board a ship. Such extreme displays of anxiety are becoming frighteningly common in our society. They usually are related to an unfounded fear—so overwhelming and so overpowering—that it clutches a person's heart, makes it beat faster, produces chills or perspiration, and the person feels completely unable to cope with the moment.

One lady wrote grippingly of her experience in an article titled "I Was a Prisoner of Panic Attacks." She begins, "While interviewing with my prospective employer, something terrifying happened. The windowless room where the interview took place closed in around me, the air became thin. My throat tightened and the rushing in my head became deafening. All I could think was, *I've got to get out.* My mind and heart raced for what seemed an eternity as I feigned composure. Somehow, I made it through the meeting without giving my interviewer a clue I had been seconds away from fleeing his office or passing out on the spot.... I endured a rush of the fight-or-flight instinct one usually experiences in life-threatening situations."[1] The reality, however, was that she wasn't in a life-threatening situation.

Anxiety is, at its core, an inappropriate response in light of the circumstances—very different from the cares and concerns in life that cause people to attend to business in a responsible way. Stress and pressure, instead of being things to avoid, strengthen us to accomplish the challenges God sets before us in life. The apostle Paul wrote that apart from the unrelenting external pressures he had to face, such as persecution, hardship, and imprisonment, he also had daily upon him the internal pressure "of concern for all the churches" (2 Cor. 11:28). In spite of that, he had room in his heart to feel the anxiety of others, for he went on to write, "Who is weak without my being weak? Who is led into sin without my intense concern?" (v. 29). He wouldn't have had it any other way, though. In fact, that kind of response to pressure is what Paul looked for in those who would serve with him. Note how he commended Timothy to the Philippian church: "I have no one else of kindred spirit who will genuinely be concerned for your welfare" (Phil. 2:20; cf. 1 Cor. 4:17).

Anyone who knows and loves Jesus Christ is capable of handling pressure like that. The wrong way to handle the stresses of life is to worry about them. Jesus said three times, "Do not be anxious" (Matt. 6:25, 31, 34). Paul later reiterated, "Be anxious for nothing" (Phil. 4:6). Worry at any time is a sin because it violates the clear biblical command.

We allow our daily concerns to turn into worry and therefore sin when our thoughts become focused on changing the future instead of doing our best to handle our present circumstances. Such thoughts are unproductive. They end up controlling us—though it should be the other way around—and cause us to neglect other responsibilities and relationships. That brings on legitimate feelings of guilt. If we don't deal with those feelings in a productive manner by getting back on track with our duties in life, we'll lose hope instead of finding answers. Anxiety, left unresolved, can debilitate one's mind and body—and even lead to panic attacks.

I am concerned about the solutions some Christians offer to the problem of anxiety. A survey of the books put out on the topic by evangelical publishing houses is telling. Most are formulaic, anecdotal, or psychological in orientation. They contain a lot of nice stories, but not many references to Scripture. When Scripture is employed, it is often incidental and without regard for its context. Scriptural concepts are often boiled down to single terms and presented something like this: "If you do [term 1] and [term 2], then God must do [term 3]."

Even more troubling to me than that superficial approach is the disdainful attitude that Scripture, apart from modern psychology, is inadequate for dealing with anxiety and life's other woes. It contradicts the biblical truth that our Lord Jesus Christ, through His divine power, "has granted to us everything pertaining to life and godliness, through the true knowledge of Him who called us by His own glory and excellence" (2 Peter 1:3). My concern over this issue prompted me to write *Our Sufficiency in Christ*.[2]

The potential danger of believers being encouraged to take a psychological approach to anxiety became especially clear to me as I read of a young Christian lady named Gloria. She sought counseling after years of worrying about her weight. She submitted herself to a well-known Christian clinic in Dallas and began extensive therapy. Because the clinic advertised on a local Christian radio station and was named after men who wrote books widely available in Christian bookstores, Gloria assumed it was a safe place for a Baptist minister's daughter to place her trust. It was the beginning of a nightmare that eventually led to her "remembering" a variety of bizarre, unspeakable crimes her parents had supposedly committed against her and accusing them in court.

*D Magazine* in Dallas picked up the story and reported it in depth.[3] They discovered there was no independent evidence to corroborate any elements of Gloria's story and that Gloria seemed to have been programmed with the perceived expectations and suggestions of her therapist, whose records showed he had counseled a string of patients with similar "memories."

One of the most shameful tragedies in life is that some children are abused by their parents, but there is absolutely no evidence that such a horror is tucked away into the far reaches of the mind, accessible only by a specially trained therapist. "Amnesia is not a common thing in post-traumatic stress disorder," explains one expert quoted by *D Magazine*. "The opposite is the case: There's a preoccupation with the event."[4] Gloria succumbed to the power of suggestion and paid a terrible price. *D Magazine* concludes, "Years after placing her trust in Christian psychologists to help her lose weight, she weighs more than ever. And Gloria's memories of her childhood have become distorted into a vision of a hell on earth."[5] She is totally alienated from the people she needs most because she has been led to believe lies about them. Her anxiety is unrelieved. What a frightening end to a young woman's quest to end worries about her weight!

The moral of the story is to be careful how you deal with your worries and to discern the kind of counsel you receive. See what you think about this advice from a contemporary Christian book:

> We suggest setting aside fifteen minutes in the morning and another fifteen minutes in the evening for active worry. If concerns surface during other times of the day, the person should jot them down on a card and vow to deal with them during the designated period. Worry-free living involves confining the natural worry we all feel into a designated time slot of only 1 percent of a twelve-hour day.[6]

Remember what Jesus and Paul said about worry? They didn't suggest we do it twice a day; they commanded us not to do it at all. The suggestion above makes about as much sense as prescribing a time limit for lascivious thoughts or any other sin that comes "naturally" to sinners!

Please don't misunderstand me: I am not against all forms of counseling. Although I have been compelled to warn about counseling that calls itself Christian but uses unbiblical means to solve spiritual problems such as anxiety, I am agonizingly aware of people's deep need to know what Scripture says about the difficulties they face. That's why I am an avid proponent of biblical, spiritual counseling. There is a great need within the church for gifted, qualified, caring people to come alongside those who are anxious, guilt ridden, depressed, or fearful. Within my own church we started a ministry that trains our members in biblical counseling so we can lovingly help one another apply scriptural solutions to our problems.

It takes time to think through important issues. To tackle anxiety in a biblical fashion, first we need to know the primary Scripture passages on the topic. Then we need to consider those passages in their context, not merely cite and recite them unthinkingly or use them as props for a nice story or a suggested behavior-modifying technique. As a person "thinks within himself, so he is" (Prov. 23:7).

As we realign our thinking on anxiety with what God says about it in His Word and why, we will be different people. We will be ready to apply His precious Word to our hearts. We won't just know we're not to worry; we will have confidence and success in doing something about it. And we can be aggressive in our approach. I've titled this book *Anxious for Nothing* because I want you to know you can overcome your anxieties. Each chapter and a special appendix at the end will show you specific biblical ways you can do just that. I trust you will find them practical, enabling you to say with the psalmist:

> When I said, "My foot is slipping,"
> Your love, O LORD, supported me.
> When anxiety was great within me,
> Your consolation brought joy to my soul.
> (Ps. 94:18–19 NIV)

# 1

# Observing How God Cares for You

❧

Sir Arthur Conan Doyle's legendary detective, Sherlock Holmes, is one of the most intriguing creations of literary fiction. He is, quite simply, extraordinary. His famous cohort, Dr. John Watson, is ordinary. Watson is often erroneously portrayed as a bumbling fool, but that flies in the face of Doyle's attempt to make the average intelligent reader relate to Watson. In this celebrated interchange between Holmes and Watson, see which character you more closely resemble:

HOLMES:  You see, but you do not observe. The distinction is clear. For example, you have frequently seen the steps which lead up from the hall to this room.

Watson:  Frequently.

Holmes:     How often?

Watson:     Well, some hundreds of times.

Holmes:     Then how many are there?

Watson:     How many? I don't know.

Holmes:     Quite so! You have not observed. And
            yet you have seen. That is just my
            point. Now, I know that there are sev-
            enteen steps, because I have both seen
            and observed.[1]

Most of us probably don't know how many steps we regularly ascend each day and therefore relate to Watson. But
here Holmes is making a point similar to the one Jesus makes
in Matthew 6:25–34. There Jesus directly addresses the topic
of worry, telling us what to do about it and why. Like
Holmes, Jesus says we need to take a good look around us
and observe or think deeply about the meaning behind what
we see. This is what Jesus tells us to ponder if we want to be
free from worry:

For this reason I say to you, do not be anxious
for your life, as to what you shall eat, or what
you shall drink; nor for your body, as to what
you shall put on. Is not life more than food, and
the body than clothing? *Look at the birds* of the
air, that they do not sow, neither do they reap,
nor gather into barns; and yet your heavenly
Father feeds them. Are you not worth much
more than they? And which of you by being
anxious can add a single cubit to his life's span?
And why are you anxious about clothing?

*Observe* how *the lilies* of the field grow; they do not toil nor do they spin, yet I say to you that even Solomon in all his glory did not clothe himself like one of these. But if God so arrays the grass of the field, which is alive today and tomorrow is thrown into the furnace, will He not much more do so for you, O men of little faith? Do not be anxious then, saying, "What shall we eat?" or "What shall we drink?" or, "With what shall we clothe ourselves?" For all these things the Gentiles eagerly seek; for your heavenly Father knows that you need all these things. But seek first His kingdom, and His righteousness; and all these things shall be added to you. Therefore do not be anxious for tomorrow; for tomorrow will care for itself. Each day has enough trouble of its own.

The often-repeated phrase "Do not be anxious" is the theme. The Lord is issuing a cease and desist order against anxiety based upon the sovereign care of a loving and omnipotent God.

## EXPRESSIONS OF WORRY

We all have to admit that worry is a common temptation in life. It is a favorite pastime for many. It can occupy a person's thoughts for a great portion of the day. However, worry cruelly inflicts a severe toll. But far beyond the need to avoid its psychological and physiological effects is the reality that Jesus commands us not to do it, thus making it clear that worry is a sin. The Christian who worries is really thinking, *God, I know You mean well by what You say, but I'm not sure You can pull it off.* Anxiety is blatant distrust of the power and love of God. In spite of its lack of subtlety, we fall into it so easily and so often.

The word *worry* comes from the Old English term *wyrgan*, which means "to choke" or "strangle." That's appropriate since worry strangles the mind, which is the seat of our emotions. The word even fits the notion of a panic attack.

We're not much different from the people to whom Jesus spoke. They worried about what they were going to eat, drink, and wear. And if you want to legitimize your worry, what better way than to think, *Well, after all, I'm not worrying about extravagant things; I'm just worrying about the basics.* But that is forbidden for the Christian.

As you read through the Scriptures, one thing you learn is that God wants His children preoccupied with Him, not with the mundane, passing things of this world. He says, "Set your mind on the things above, not on the things that are on earth" (Col. 3:2). To free us to do that He says, "Don't worry about the basics. I'll take care of that." A basic principle of spiritual life is that we are not earthbound people. Fully trusting our heavenly Father dispells anxiety. And the more we know about Him, the more we will trust Him.

Many rich people worry about necessities—that's why they stockpile so much of their resources as a hedge against the future. Many poor people also worry about life's essentials, but they aren't in a position to stockpile. It's just as well that they can't because stockpiling basically is an attempt to determine one's own destiny apart from faith and trust in God. Even Christians can make that mistake.

Believers are commanded to be financially responsible and care for their families (1 Tim. 5:8). Scripture does not imply that having a savings account, investing extra money, or owning insurance shows a lack of trust in God. Such provisions from the Lord are reasonable safeguards for the average person in any complex, modern society. However, they ought to be balanced with Jesus' command to "seek first His kingdom, and His righteousness" (Matt. 6:33) and to "lay up for yourselves treasures in heaven" (v. 20 KJV). We are not to lavish on ourselves what God has given us for the accomplishment of His holy purposes.

I believe in wise planning, but if after doing all you are able to, you still are fearful of the future, the Lord says, "Don't worry." He promised to provide all your needs, and He will: "My God shall supply all your needs according to His riches in glory in Christ Jesus" (Phil. 4:19). That is His concern, not yours.

## What Jesus Says about Worry

In Matthew 6:25 Jesus says, "Do not be anxious for your life, as to what you shall eat, or what you shall drink; nor for your body, as to what you shall put on. Is not life more than food, and the body than clothing?" The tense in the Greek text is properly translated, "Stop worrying." The tense in verse 31 is different, however, and means, "Don't start worrying." Thus Jesus brackets our passage with this meaning: If you are worrying, quit; if you haven't started, don't.

The Greek word for "life" is *psuchē*. It has to do with the fullness of earthly, physical, external life. Don't be anxious about this temporal world—and the food, clothing, and shelter associated with it. Jesus said previously, "Where your treasure is, there will your heart be also" (Matt. 6:21). Focusing on earthly treasures produces earthly affections. It blinds our spiritual vision and draws us away from serving God. That's why God promises to provide what we need.

As children of God we have a single goal—treasure in heaven; a single vision—God's purposes; and a single Master—God, not money (vv. 19–24). Therefore, we must not let ourselves become preoccupied with the mundane things of this world—"what [we] shall eat, or what [we] shall drink" (v. 25).

Perhaps in American society such a warning seems a bit obscure. After all, there's a market of some sort on practically every corner. We've got so much water in our homes we never think about it. But then again, maybe some conservation prophet of doom comes along and says we're running out of food and water in America, and maybe we do worry a little.

To appreciate the impact of what Jesus said to His hearers, imagine what it would be like to live in a less plentiful country. If you were living in Palestine at Jesus' time, you might have cause for concern. There were times when the snows didn't come to the mountains, and as a result the streams didn't run. Sometimes a plague of locusts would devour the crops, bringing about famine in the land. When there was famine, there was also no income. And when there was no income, no one could purchase clothing and other necessities.

Jesus' saying not to worry about such things is especially powerful in the context of His day. Certainly that is an indictment of our own worry about life's basics. Jesus then asks rhetorically, "Is not life more than food, and the body than clothing?" (v. 25). Of course it is, but you wouldn't know it judging by what's advertised today and what people seem to feel they need to be pursuing.

So many in our society are totally consumed with the body—they decorate it, fix it up, clothe it, put it in a nice car, send it off to a nice house, stuff it full of food, sit it in a comfortable chair, hang a bunch of jewelry all over it, take it out on a boat, let it swim, teach it to ski, take it on a cruise, and so on. But life is not contained in those things; it transcends all externals. Life comes from God—and the fullness of life from Jesus Christ.

## WHY HE SAYS IT

Jesus gives us, His children, three reasons for not worrying about this life: It is unnecessary because of our Father, it is uncharacteristic because of our faith, and it is unwise because of our future.

### WORRY IS UNNECESSARY BECAUSE OF OUR FATHER

It is unnecessary to worry about finances, the basics of life, and what we eat or drink or wear because of who our heavenly Father is. Have we forgotten what He is like? My children never worried about where they were going to get their next meal or whether they would have clothes, a bed, or something to drink. Such thoughts never entered their minds because they knew enough about me to know I would provide for them—and I don't come close to being as faithful as God. Yet how often we fail to believe that God is going to provide for us as well as the average earthly father.

If your concept of God is right and you see Him as Owner, Controller, and Provider, and beyond that as your loving Father, then you know you have nothing to worry about. Jesus said, "What man is there among you, when his son shall ask him for a loaf, will give him a stone? Or if he shall ask for a fish, he will not give him a snake, will he? If you then, being evil, know how to give good gifts to your children, how much more shall your Father who is in heaven give what is good to those who ask Him!" (Matt. 7:9–11).

Since all things come under God's control, rest assured He controls those things on behalf of His children. Jesus illustrates that with three observations from nature.

### God always feeds his creatures

In Matthew 6:26 Jesus says, "Look at the birds of the air, that they do not sow, neither do they reap, nor gather into barns; and yet your heavenly Father feeds them. Are you not worth much more than they?" I can imagine the Lord standing on a hillside up in Galilee looking over the beautiful north end of the sea, the breeze rippling across the water, the sun bright in the sky. Since that part of the Sea of Galilee was known as a crossroads of bird migration, perhaps Jesus saw a flock fly by as He spoke.

He wants us to think about birds. Here's one observation: Birds don't get together and say, "We've got to come up with a strategy to keep ourselves alive." They have no self-consciousness or ability to reason. But God has planted within them the instinct or divine capacity to find what is necessary to live. God doesn't just create life; He also sustains life.

Job 38:41 and Psalm 147:9 tell us that baby birds cry out to God for their food. Jesus tells us that even though they don't sow or reap or gather surplus into barns, their heavenly Father hears and provides for them. Now that isn't an excuse for idleness. You won't see a bird standing out on the edge of a tree with its mouth wide open. Perhaps you've noticed: It never rains worms! God feeds birds through the instinct that tells them where to find food. They work hard for it. They're always busy searching, gobbling up little insects, preparing their nests, caring for their young, teaching them to fly, pushing them out of the nest at the right time, migrating with the seasons, and so on.

All this work is to be done if they are going to eat, yet they never overdo it. Not even in your strangest dream would a bird say, "I'm going to build bigger nests. I'm going to store more worms. I'm going to say to myself, 'Bird, eat, drink, and be merry.'" Birds work within the framework of God's design and never overindulge themselves. They get fat only when people put them in cages.

Birds don't worry about where they are going to find food; they just go about their business until they find it, and they always do because God is looking out for them. Birds have no reason to worry, and if they don't, what are you worrying for? Jesus put it this way: "Are not two sparrows sold for a cent? And yet not one of them will fall to the ground apart from your Father. But the very hairs of your head are all numbered. Therefore do not fear; you are of more value than many sparrows" (Matt. 10:29–31).

Are you not much better than a bird? No bird was ever created in the image of God; no bird was ever designed to be a joint heir with Jesus Christ; no bird was ever prepared a place in heaven in the Father's house. If God sustains the life of a bird, don't you think He will take care of you? Life is a gift from God. If God gives you the greater gift of life itself, don't you think He will give you the lesser gift of sustaining that life? Of course He will, so don't worry about it.

Keep in mind, of course, that like a bird, we have to work because God has designed that man should earn his bread by the sweat of his brow (Gen. 3:19). If we don't work, it is not fitting that we eat (2 Thess. 3:10). Just as God provides for the birds through their instinct, so God provides for man through his effort.

Some people fear we are running out of resources. I read a brochure from the United States Department of Agriculture titled *Is the World Facing Starvation?* that gives these answers to two commonly asked questions:

- "Is the world's food supply large enough to meet everyone's minimum needs?" Answer: "The world has more than enough food to feed every man, woman, and child in it. If the world's food supply had been evenly divided and distributed among the world's population for the last 18 years, each person would have received more than the minimum number of calories. From 1960 to the present, world food grain production never dropped below 103 percent of the minimum requirements and averaged 108 percent between 1973 and 1977.... If a system existed today to distribute grains equitably, the world's 4 billion people would have available about one-fifth more grain per person than the 2.7 billion people had 25 years ago."[2]
- "Hasn't the amount of food produced per person been dropping in the developing countries of the world over the last 25 years?" Answer: "This is a common misconception. Food production in the developing countries has been increasing.... World per capita food production declined only twice

in the last 25 years.... Production of grain,
the primary food for most of the world's
people, rose from 290 kilograms per person
during the early 1950s to an average of 360
kilograms some forty years later, about a 25
percent increase."[3]

Obviously some of the statistics have changed, but the
essential fact remains the same: There is more food on earth
than ever. When God says He will provide, He means just
that. Every time you see a bird, let it serve as a reminder of
God's abundant provision. May it stop cold any worry you
might have.

*Worry is unable to accomplish anything productive*
Jesus gives another practical observation that highlights the
folly of worry: "Which of you by being anxious can add ...
to his life's span?" (Matt. 6:27). Not only will you not
lengthen your life by worrying, but you will probably
shorten it. Charles Mayo, cofounder of the Mayo Clinic,
made the observation that worry adversely affects the circu-
latory system, heart, glands, and entire nervous system. In
the medical journal *American Mercury* Mayo said he never
knew anyone who died of overwork, but he knew many who
died of worry. You can worry yourself to death, but you'll
never worry yourself into a longer life.

We live in a day when people are in a panic to lengthen
their lives. They have an excessive interest in vitamins, health
spas, diet, and exercise. God, however, has previously determined how long we shall live. Job 14:5 says of man, "His
days are determined, the number of his months is with Thee,
and his limits Thou hast set so that he cannot pass." Does

that mean we should disregard sensible advice about our diet and exercise? Of course not: It will increase the quality of our lives, but there's no guarantee about the quantity. When I exercise and eat right, my body and brain work better and I feel better all around, but I'm not going to kid myself that by jogging in the neighborhood every day and eating hefty quantities of complex carbohydrates that I'm going to force God to let me live longer.

To worry about how long you are going to live and how to add years onto your life is to distrust God. If you give Him your life and are obedient to Him, He will give you the fullness of days. You will experience life to the fullest when you live it to the glory of God. No matter how long or short, it will be wonderful.

### God arrays even the meadows in splendor

Jesus gives another illustration from nature on why not to worry: "Why are you anxious about clothing? Observe how the lilies of the field grow; they do not toil nor do they spin, yet I say to you that even Solomon in all his glory did not clothe himself like one of these. But if God so arrays the grass of the field, which is alive today and tomorrow is thrown into the furnace, will He not much more do so for you, O men of little faith?" (Matt. 6:28–30).

For some people, the most important place in their whole world is the closet. Instead of being afraid they won't have anything to wear—a major concern in biblical times—these jaded individuals fear not being able to look their best! Lusting after costly clothes is a common sin in our society.

Whenever I walk through a shopping mall, I am overwhelmed by how much stuff is hanging on the racks. I don't know how those stores can sustain their inventory. We have made a god out of fashion. We indulge in a spending spree to drape our bodies with things that have nothing to do with the beauty of character: "Let not your adornment be external only—braiding the hair, and wearing gold jewelry, and putting on dresses; but let it be the hidden person of the heart, with the imperishable quality of a gentle and quiet spirit, which is precious in the sight of God" (1 Peter 3:3–4).

If you want to talk about fancy clothing, though, Jesus tells us that the best this world has to offer doesn't even compare to "the lilies of the field" (Matt. 6:28). That's a general term for all the wildflowers that graced the rolling hills of Galilee, such as anemones, gladiolus, narcissus, and poppies. "They do not toil nor do they spin" (v. 28)—you won't find one making fancy thread to drape over itself and saying, "I've been scarlet for two whole days now. I think I'd like to be blue tomorrow."

Look at the simplest flowers around you: There is a free and easy beauty about them. You can take the most glorious garment ever made for a great monarch like Solomon, put it under a microscope, and it will look like sackcloth. But if you likewise examine the petal of a flower, you could become lost in the wonder of what you would see. If you've ever taken a good look at a flower, you know there is a texture, form, design, substance, and color that man with all his ingenuity cannot come close to duplicating.

So what is the point? That "if God so arrays the grass of the field, which is alive today and tomorrow is thrown into the furnace, will He not much more do so for you?" (Matt. 6:30). Wildflowers have a very short life span. People would gather dead batches of them as a cheap source of fuel for their portable cooking furnaces. A God who would lavish such beauty on temporary fire fodder certainly will provide the necessary clothing for His eternal children. An anonymous poem expresses this lesson simply:

> Said the wildflower to the sparrow:
> "I should really like to know
> Why these anxious human beings
> Rush about and worry so."
>
> Said the sparrow to the wildflower:
> "Friend, I think that it must be
> That they have no heavenly Father,
> Such as cares for you and me."

## WORRY IS UNCHARACTERISTIC BECAUSE OF OUR FAITH

If you worry, what kind of faith do you manifest? "Little faith," according to Jesus (Matt. 6:30). If you are a child of God, you by definition have a heavenly Father. To act like you don't, nervously asking, "What shall I eat? What shall I drink? With what shall I clothe myself?" is to act like an unbeliever in God's eyes (vv. 31–32).

Christians who worry believe God can redeem them, break the shackles of Satan, take them from hell to heaven, put them into His kingdom, and give them eternal life; but they just don't think He can get them through the next couple of days. That is pretty ridiculous. We can believe God for the greater gift and then stumble and not believe Him for the lesser one.

### The worrier strikes out at God

Someone might say, "Why make a big deal out of worry? It's just a trivial sin." No, it is not. I suspect a majority of mental illnesses and some physical illnesses are directly related to worry. Worry is devastating. But more important than what worry does to you is what it does to God. When you worry, you are saying in effect, "God, I just don't think I can trust You." Worry strikes a blow at the person and character of God.

### The worrier disbelieves Scripture
It breaks my heart to hear some Christians say, "I believe in the inerrancy of Scripture," but then live as perpetual worriers. They are saying one thing out of one side of their mouth and another thing out of the other. It is incongruous to say how much we believe the Bible and then worry about God fulfilling what He says in it.

### The worrier is mastered by circumstances
When you or I worry, we are choosing to be mastered by our circumstances instead of by the truth of God. The hardships and trials of life pale in comparison to the greatness of our salvation. Jesus wants us to realize it doesn't make sense to believe God can save us from eternal hell but not help us in the practical matters of life. The apostle Paul reflects a similar desire in Ephesians 1:18–19: "I pray that the eyes of your heart may be enlightened, so that you may know what is the hope of His calling, what are the riches of the glory of His inheritance in the saints, and what is the surpassing greatness of His power toward us who believe." When you catch yourself worrying, go back to Scripture and have your eyes opened again.

### The worrier distrusts God
When we worry, we are not trusting our heavenly Father. That means we don't know Him well enough. Take heart—there's

an effective remedy: Study the Word of God to find out who He really is and how He has supplied the needs of His people in the past. That will build confidence for the future. Stay fresh in the Word every day so that God is in your mind. Otherwise Satan is apt to move into the vacuum and tempt you to worry about something. Instead, let God's track record in Scripture and in your own life assure you that worry is needless because of God's bounty, senseless because of God's promise, useless because of its impotence to do anything productive, and faithless because it is characteristic of unbelievers.

## WORRY IS UNWISE BECAUSE OF OUR FUTURE

Jesus said, "Therefore do not be anxious for tomorrow; for tomorrow will care for itself. Each day has enough trouble of its own" (Matt. 6:34). He was saying, "Don't worry about the future. Even though it will have its share of problems, they have a way of working themselves out at the time. Just deal with them as they come, for there's no way to solve them in advance." Providing for tomorrow is good, but worrying about tomorrow is sin because God is the God of tomorrow just like He is the God of today. Lamentations 3:23 tells us His mercies "are new every morning." He feeds us like He fed the children of Israel—with just enough manna for the day.

Worry paralyzes its victim, making him or her too upset to accomplish anything productive. It will seek to do that to you by taking you mentally into tomorrow until you find something to worry about. Refuse to go along for the ride. The Lord says you have enough to deal with today. Apply today's resources to today's needs or you will lose today's joy.

Lack of joy is a sin for the child of God. By worrying about tomorrow, many believers miss the victory God would give them today. That is not fair to Him. *"This* is the day the LORD has made; let us rejoice and be glad in it" (Ps. 118:24 NIV). God gives you the glorious gift of life today; live in the light and full joy of that day, using the resources God supplies. Don't push yourself into the future and forfeit the day's joy over some tomorrow that may never happen. Today is all you really have, for God permits none of us to live in tomorrow until it turns into today. Jay Adams, who has written excellent materials on counseling those who struggle with anxiety and other sins, adds this:

> Tomorrow always belongs to God.... Whenever
> we try to take hold of it, we try to steal what
> belongs to Him. Sinners want what is not theirs
> to have, and thereby destroy themselves. God has
> given us only today. He strongly forbids us to
> become concerned about what might happen....
> Worriers not only want what has been forbidden,
> but also fail to use what has been given to them.[4]

Realize God gives you strength one day at a time. He gives you what you need when you need it. He doesn't encumber you with excess baggage. Perhaps your worst fear is how you'd handle a loved one's death. Let me assure you as a pastor who's kept watch over many Christians finding themselves in this situation, this is the attitude I most often encounter: "It is so wonderful how God has sustained me! Of course I miss my loved one, but I feel such incredible strength and confidence and a gladness in my heart that he is with the Lord." God gives us His grace in the hour we need it. If we worry about the future now, we double our pain without having the grace to deal with it.

"Jesus Christ is the same yesterday and today ... and forever" (Heb. 13:8). That means He will be doing the same thing tomorrow that He was doing yesterday. If you have any question about the future, look at the past. Did He sustain you then? He will sustain you in the future.

## REPLACING WORRY WITH THE RIGHT FOCUS

This is what Jesus says to you today: "Seek first His kingdom, and His righteousness; and all these things shall be added to you" (Matt. 6:33). In other words, move your thoughts up to the divine level, and God will take care of all your physical needs. God wants to free His children from being preoccupied with the mundane. Colossians 3:2 says as directly as possible, "Set your mind on the things above, not on the things that are on earth." Therefore a materialistic Christian is a contradiction in terms.

The Greek word *prōtos* ("first") means "first in a line of more than one option." Of all the priorities of life, seeking God's kingdom is number one. It is doing what you can to promote God's rule over His creation. That includes seeking Christ's rule to be manifest in your life through "righteousness and peace and joy in the Holy Spirit" (Rom. 14:17). When the world sees those virtues in your life instead of worry, it's evidence that the kingdom of God is there. You can say, "I want to tell people about Jesus so they can be saved," but if your life is marked by anxiety and fear, they will not believe you have anything they want. They are certainly going to question the power of God.

Perhaps you already are painfully aware of your less-than-perfect testimony and would do anything to root out your shortcomings. Although in the context of addressing irrational fears, Jay Adams offers this wise caution that applies to any sin you lament in yourself:

> God wants you to seek to please Him first, and think about the problem of fear secondly. That is why when speaking of worry (a lesser form of fear), in Matthew 6:33 He commands "Seek *first* the kingdom of God and His righteousness." If you put anything else first—even the desire to rid yourself of a terrifying fear—you will discover that you will fail to achieve either goal. God will not take second place, even to a legitimate concern to be free of fear.[5]

What is your heart's preoccupation? Are you more concerned with the kingdom or with the things of this world? Love for what this world can offer is an especially tempting sin in our society. You wouldn't be alone if you as a Christian have been tempted by it. The Russian playwright Anton Chekhov cleverly stripped the world of its allure in his short story "The Bet." In it a poor attorney makes a bet with a frivolous wealthy banker for two million dollars if he voluntarily submits himself to solitary confinement for fifteen years under the banker's supervision. In the first year the books he sent for were mostly of a light character. In the second year the prisoner asked only for the classics. Later on he began zealously studying languages, music, philosophy, and history. By the tenth year the prisoner sat immovably at his table and read nothing but the Gospels. Theology and histories of religion followed.

The night before he was due to collect the two million, the prisoner wrote this to his captor:

> With a clear conscience I tell you, as before God, who beholds me, that I despise freedom and life and health, and all that in your books is called the good things of the world.
>
> For fifteen years I have been intently studying earthly life. It is true I have not seen the earth nor men, but in your books I have drunk fragrant wine, I have sung songs, I have hunted stags and ... have loved women.... Beauties as ethereal as clouds, created by the magic of your poets and geniuses, have visited me at night, and have whispered in my ears wonderful tales that have set my brain in a whirl....
>
> Your books have given me wisdom. All that the unresting thought of man has created in the ages is compressed into a small compass in my brain. I know that I am wiser than all of you.
>
> [Yet] I despise your books, I despise wisdom and the blessings of this world. It is all worthless, fleeting, illusory, and deceptive, like a mirage. You may be proud, wise, and fine, but death will wipe you off the face of the earth....
>
> You have lost your reason and taken the wrong path. You have taken lies for truth, and hideousness for beauty.... I marvel at you who exchange heaven for earth....
>
> To prove to you in action how I despise all that you live by, I renounce the two millions of

which I once dreamed as of paradise and which
now I despise.[6]


That's an example of learning the hard way. We as believers don't need to do that. Our Lord "gives grace and glory; no good thing does He withhold from those who walk uprightly" (Ps. 84:11). Don't be anxious for the goods of this world—or anything else for that matter. As Sherlock Holmes would say, don't just see but observe. And remember what Jesus told you to observe: abundant evidence all around you of God's lavish care for the needs of His beloved.

# AVOIDING ANXIETY
# THROUGH PRAYER

ᏟᏎ

J ust as Matthew 6 is Jesus' great statement on worry, Philippians 4 is the apostle Paul's charter on how to avoid anxiety. Those passages are the most comprehensive portions of Scripture dealing with our topic and therefore are foundational to understanding how God feels about anxiety and why He feels that way. The teaching is clear, compelling, and direct. In Philippians 4:6–9, Paul issued these series of commands:

> Be anxious for nothing, but in everything by
> prayer and supplication with thanksgiving let your
> requests be made known to God. And the peace
> of God, which surpasses all comprehension, shall
> guard your hearts and your minds in Christ Jesus.

> Finally, brethren, whatever is true, whatever is
> honorable, whatever is right, whatever is pure,
> whatever is lovely, whatever is of good repute, if
> there is any excellence and if anything worthy of
> praise, let your mind dwell on these things. The
> things you have learned and received and heard
> and seen in me, practice these things; and the God
> of peace shall be with you.

Paul straightaway said not to worry, but he doesn't leave us there. He helps us fill the vacuum by directing us toward positive steps: right praying, right thinking, and right action. The best way to eliminate a bad habit is to replace it with a good one, and few habits are as bad as worrying. The foremost way to avoid it is through prayer. Right thinking and action are the next logical steps, but it all begins with prayer.

### REACT TO PROBLEMS WITH THANKFUL PRAYER

Paul said, "In everything by prayer and supplication with thanksgiving let your requests be made known to God" (v. 6). This teaching tells us how to pray with gratitude. The Greek terms Paul used refer to specific petitions made to God in the midst of difficulty.

Instead of praying to God with feelings of doubt, discouragement, or discontent, we are to approach Him with a thankful attitude before we utter even one word. We can do that with sincerity when we realize that God promises not to allow anything to happen to us that will be too much for us to bear (1 Cor. 10:13), to work out everything for our good in the end (Rom. 8:28), and to "perfect, confirm, strengthen and establish" us in the midst of our suffering (1 Peter 5:10).

These are key principles for living the Christian life. Go beyond memorizing them to letting them be the grid through which you automatically interpret all that happens to you. Know that all your difficulties are within God's purpose, and thank Him for His available power and promises.

Being thankful will release you from fear and worry. It is a tangible demonstration of trusting your situation to God's sovereign control. (And it is easy to do,) since there are so many blessings to be thankful for: knowing that God will supply all our needs (Phil. 4:19), that He stays closely in touch with our lives (Ps. 139:3), that He cares about us (1 Peter 5:7), that all power belongs to Him (Ps. 62:11), that He is making us more and more like Christ (Rom. 8:29; Phil. 1:6), and that no detail escapes Him (Ps. 147:5).

The prophet Jonah reacted with thankful prayer when a great fish swallowed him (Jonah 2:1, 9). If you suddenly found yourself swimming in a fish's gastric juices, how do you think you'd react? Maybe you'd cry out, "God, what are You doing? Where are You? Why is this happening to me?" If there were ever an excuse for panic, surely this would be it. But no, Jonah reacted differently:

> I called out of my distress to the Lord, and He
> answered me.... Thou hadst cast me into the
> deep, into the heart of the seas.... I have been
> expelled from Thy sight.... Water encompassed
> me to the very soul, the great deep engulfed
> me, weeds were wrapped around my head. I
> descended to the roots of the mountains....
> While I was fainting away, I remembered the
> Lord; and my prayer came to Thee, into Thy
> holy temple. Those who regard vain idols

forsake their faithfulness, but I will sacrifice to
Thee with the voice of thanksgiving.... Salvation
is from the Lord. (vv. 2–9)

Although Jonah had his weaknesses, he reflected pro-
found spiritual stability in this prayer. He was confident of
God's ability to deliver him if He so chose. In the same way
the peace of God will help us be stable if we react to our circumstances, however unusual or ordinary, with thankful
prayer instead of anxiety. That's the promise of Philippians
4:7: "The peace of God, which surpasses all comprehension,
shall guard your hearts and your minds in Christ Jesus."

This precious verse promises inner calm and tranquility to
believers who pray with a thankful attitude. Notice, however,
it doesn't promise what the answer to our prayers will be.

This peace "surpasses all comprehension," which speaks
of its divine origin. It transcends human intellect, analysis,
and insight. No human counselor can give it to you because
it's a gift from God in response to gratitude and trust.

The real challenge of Christian living is not to eliminate
every uncomfortable circumstance from our lives, but to
trust our sovereign, wise, good, and powerful God in the
midst of every situation. Things that might trouble us such
as the way we look, the way others treat us, or where we live
or work can actually be sources of strength, not weakness.

Jesus said to His disciples, "These things I have spoken to
you, that in Me you may have peace. In the world you have
tribulation, but take courage; I have overcome the world"
(John 16:33). As disciples of Christ, we need to accept the
fact that we live in an imperfect world and allow God to do
His perfect work in us. Our Lord will give us His peace as we
confidently entrust ourselves to His care.

The peace of God "shall guard your hearts and your minds in Christ Jesus" (Phil. 4:7). John Bunyan's allegory *The Holy War* illustrates how this peace guards the believer's heart from anxiety, doubt, fear, and distress. In it Mr. God's-Peace was appointed to guard the city of Mansoul. As long as Mr. God's-Peace ruled, Mansoul enjoyed harmony, happiness, joy, and health. However, Prince Emmanuel (Christ) went away because Mansoul grieved him. Consequently, Mr. God's-Peace resigned his commission and chaos resulted.

The believer who doesn't live in the confidence of God's sovereignty will lack God's peace and be left to the chaos of a troubled heart. But our confident trust in the Lord will allow us to thank Him in the midst of trials because we have God's peace on duty to protect our hearts.

During World War II, an armed German freighter picked up a missionary whose ship had been torpedoed. He was put into the hold. For a while he was too terrified to even close his eyes. Sensing the need to adjust his perspective, he tells us how he got through the night: "I began communing with the Lord. He reminded me of His word in the 121st Psalm: 'My help cometh from the LORD, which made heaven and earth. He will not suffer thy foot to be moved: he that keepeth thee will not slumber. Behold, he … shall neither slumber nor sleep' (vv. 2–4 KJV).... So I said, 'Lord there isn't really any use for both of us to stay awake tonight. If You are going to keep watch, I'll thank Thee for some sleep!'"[1] He replaced his fear and anxiety with thankful prayer, and the peace of God that resulted enabled him to sleep soundly. You too will enjoy peace and rest when you cultivate the habit of looking to God with a grateful attitude.

## FOCUS ON GODLY VIRTUES

Prayer is our chief means of avoiding anxiety. After Paul said not to be anxious (Phil. 4:6), he added two complete sentences specifying how we're to pray and what the benefits will be. The English text, reflective of the Greek, launches into a new paragraph on godly thinking and practices. Philippians 4 is often oversimplified and misrepresented as a mere grocery list on how to deal with worry, but it is much more than that. As believers, we're to leave the sin of worry behind with our prayers and gradually become different people through new ways of thinking and acting. Let's now explore these next steps beyond worry.

Paul wrote these words: "Whatever is true, whatever is honorable, whatever is right, whatever is pure, whatever is lovely, whatever is of good repute, if there is any excellence and if anything worthy of praise, let your mind dwell on these things" (v. 8). As mentioned earlier, we are the products of our thinking. According to Proverbs 23:7, "As [a person] thinks within himself, so he is." Unfortunately, many psychologists believe an individual can find stability by recalling his past sins, hurts, and abuses. That kind of thinking has infiltrated Christianity. The apostle Paul, however, said to focus only on what is right and honorable, not on the sins of darkness (cf. Eph. 5:12).

### HOW WE THINK

To give you some background, let's survey what Scripture says about our thinking patterns before, at, and after salvation.

Describing unredeemed humanity, Paul wrote: "As they did not see fit to acknowledge God any longer, God gave them over to a depraved mind" (Rom. 1:28). Once, our minds were corrupt. Worse, our minds were also blind, for "the god of this world has blinded the minds of the unbelieving" (2 Cor. 4:4). As a result, our minds were engaged in futile thoughts (Eph. 4:17). Indeed, prior to salvation, our minds are "darkened in their understanding, excluded from the life of God, because of the ignorance that is in them" (v. 18). Since the mind of the nonbeliever is corrupt, it doesn't choose what is good; since it is spiritually blind, it doesn't know what is good; since its thoughts are futile, it doesn't perform what is good; and since it is ignorant, it doesn't even know what evil it is doing. What a tragic train of thought!

The ability to think clearly and correctly is a tremendous blessing from God. It all begins with the gospel, which is "the power of God for salvation" (Rom. 1:16). The Lord uses the gospel to illumine the mind of the unbeliever. In fact, Paul said that faith comes by hearing about Christ (Rom. 10:17). Salvation begins in the mind as an individual comes to realize the seriousness of sin and Christ's atoning work on his or her behalf. Jesus said, "You shall love the Lord your God with all your heart, and with all your soul, and with all your strength, and with all your mind" (Luke 10:27). Salvation requires an intelligent response: Trust in the revealed truth of God, which proves itself in life to be true and reasonable.

Recall that Jesus said, "Look at the birds of the air, that they do not sow, neither do they reap, nor gather into barns; and yet your heavenly Father feeds them. Are you not worth much more than they?" (Matt. 6:26). Martyn Lloyd-Jones, commenting on that verse, explains:

> Faith, according to our Lord's teaching ... is
> primarily thinking.... We must spend more time

in studying our Lord's lessons in observation
and deduction. The Bible is full of logic, and we
must never think of faith as something purely
mystical. We do not just sit down in an armchair
and expect marvelous things to happen to us.
That is not Christian faith. Christian faith is
essentially thinking. Look at the birds, think
about them, and draw your deductions. Look at
the grass, look at the lilies of the field, consider
them....

Faith, if you like, can be defined like this: It
is a man insisting upon thinking when everything seems determined to bludgeon and knock
him down.... The trouble with the person of
little faith is that, instead of controlling his own
thought, his thought is being controlled by
something else, and, as we put it, he goes
round and round in circles. That is the essence
of worry.... That is not thought; that is the
absence of thought, a failure to think.[2]

Some people assume worry is the result of too much
thinking. Actually, it's the result of too little thinking in the
right direction. If you know who God is and understand His
purposes, promises, and plans, it will help you not to worry.

Faith isn't psychological self-hypnosis or wishful thinking, but a reasoned response to revealed truth. When we in
faith embrace Christ as our Lord and Savior, our minds are
transformed. The Holy Spirit is at work in us, renewing us;
and we receive a new mind or way of thinking. Divine and
supernatural thoughts inject our human thought patterns.

"The thoughts of God no one knows except the Spirit of God," said Paul, but we as believers "have received, not the spirit of the world, but the Spirit who is from God, that we might know the things freely given to us by God" (1 Cor. 2:11–12). In other words, because the Holy Spirit indwells us, the very thoughts of God are available to us.

Since we still live in a fallen world, however, our renewed minds need ongoing cleansing and refreshment. Jesus said that God's chief agent for purifying our thinking is His Word (John 15:3). Paul reiterated that concept many times:

- Romans 12:1–2: "I urge you therefore, brethren, by the mercies of God, to present your bodies a living and holy sacrifice, acceptable to God, which is your spiritual service of worship. And do not be conformed to this world, but be transformed by the renewing of your mind, that you may prove what the will of God is, that which is good and acceptable and perfect."
- Ephesians 4:23: "Be renewed in the spirit of your mind."
- Colossians 3:10: "Put on the new self who is being renewed to a true knowledge according to the image of the One who created him."
- 1 Thessalonians 5:21: "Examine everything carefully; hold fast to that which is good."

The New Testament calls us to the mental discipline of right thinking. Paul said, "Set your mind on the things above, not on the things that are on earth" (Col. 3:2) In addition,

Peter said, "Gird your minds for action, keep sober in spirit, fix your hope completely on the grace to be brought to you at the revelation of Jesus Christ" (1 Peter 1:13).

Think how often Paul said in his letters, "I would not ... that ye be ignorant" (Rom. 11:25; 1 Cor. 10:1; 2 Cor. 1:8; 1 Thess. 4:13 KJV) and "know ye not" (Rom. 6:3, 16; 1 Cor. 3:16; 2 Cor. 13:5 KJV). He was concerned that we think rightly. Jesus Himself often used the term translated "think" to help His listeners have the right focus (Matt. 5:17; 18:12; 21:28; 22:42).

## WHAT WE SHOULD THINK ABOUT

What is that right focus? Dwelling on "whatever is true ... honorable ... right ... pure ... lovely ... of good repute" (Phil. 4:8).

### Truthful things

We will find what is true in God's Word. Jesus said, "Sanctify them in the truth; Thy word is truth" (John 17:17; cf. Ps. 119:151). The truth is also in Christ Himself—"just as truth is in Jesus," said Paul (Eph. 4:21). Dwelling on what is true necessitates meditating on God's Word and "fixing our eyes on Jesus the author and perfecter of [our] faith" (Heb. 12:2).

### Noble things

The Greek word that is translated "honorable" refers to what is noble, dignified, and worthy of respect. We are to dwell on whatever is worthy of awe and adoration—the sacred as opposed to the profane.

## Righteous things

The term "right" speaks of righteousness. Our thoughts are to be in perfect harmony with the eternal, unchanging, divine standard of our Holy God as revealed in Scripture. Right thinking is always consistent with God's absolute holiness.

## Pure things

"Pure" refers to something morally clean and undefiled. We are to dwell on what is clean, not soiled.

## Gracious things

The Greek term translated "lovely" occurs only here in the New Testament and means "pleasing" or "amiable." The implication is that we are to focus on whatever is kind or gracious.

## Praiseworthy things

"Honorable" predominantly refers to something worthy of veneration by believers, but "good repute" refers more to what is reputable in the world at large. This term includes universally praised virtues such as courage and respect for others.

In essence Paul was saying, "Since there are so many excellent and worthy things out there, please focus on them." Focusing on godly virtues will affect what you decide to see (such as television programs, books, or magazines) and say (perhaps to family and those at work). That's because your thinking affects your desires and behavior.

How does all that lofty teaching apply to fear and anxiety? Jay Adams gives this practical advice:

> Whenever you catch your mind wandering back into the forbidden territory (and you can be

sure that it will—more frequently at first, until
you retrain and discipline it ...) change the
direction of your thought. Do not allow yourself one conscious moment of such thought.
Instead, crisply ask God to help you to refocus
upon those things that fit into Paul's list
recorded in Philippians 4:8–9. The attitude
must grow within you that says: "So if I have a
fear experience, so what? It's unpleasant, it's
disturbing, but I'll live through it—at least I
always have before." When you honestly can
think this way without becoming anxious, you
will know that the change has been made.[3]

## Practice What's Been Preached

All this godly thinking is to lead to a practical end. Paul put
it this way: "The things you have learned and received and
heard and seen in me, practice these things; and the God of
peace shall be with you" (Phil. 4:9).

Paul's words speak of action that's repetitious or con-
tinuous. When we say someone is practicing the violin or
something else, we mean that person is working to
improve a skill. When we say a doctor or lawyer has a
practice, we are referring to his or her professional rou-
tine. Similarly, the word here refers to one's pattern of life
or conduct.

God's Word cultivates the godly attitudes, thoughts, and
actions that will keep trials and temptations from overwhelming us. To understand the relationship between the three,
consider this analogy: If a police officer sees someone who's

about to violate the law, he or she will restrain that person. Similarly, godly attitudes and thoughts produced by the Word act as police officers to restrain the flesh before it commits a crime against the standard of God's Word. But if they aren't on duty, they can't restrain the flesh, and the flesh is free to violate the law of God.

Right attitudes and thoughts must precede right practices. Only spiritual weapons will help in our warfare against the flesh (2 Cor. 10:4). By avoiding anxiety through prayer and making other such attitude adjustments, we can take "every thought captive to the obedience of Christ" (v. 5).

Pure behavior, in turn, produces spiritual peace and stability. The prophet Isaiah said, "The work of righteousness will be peace, and the service of righteousness, quietness and confidence forever" (Isa. 32:17). Similarly, James wrote, "The wisdom from above is first pure, then peaceable.... The seed whose fruit is righteousness is sown in peace by those who make peace" (James 3:17–18).

Paul said, "The things you have learned and received and heard and seen in me, practice these things" (Phil. 4:9). Paul exemplified the spiritual fruit of peace, joy, humility, faith, and gratitude. He clearly dwelled on what was true, honorable, right, pure, lovely, and of good repute. Therefore, he wasn't embarrassed to tell people who knew him well to practice what they had seen in his life.

Today we have the New Testament as the divine pattern for our conduct. In no way does that mean, however, that those who currently preach, teach, and represent the New Testament are permitted to live any way they want. Even though none of us are apostles, our lives are to be worthy of imitation or we disqualify ourselves from the ministry. Moreover, as believers we are all to prove ourselves "doers of the word, and not merely hearers" (James 1:22). Never expose yourself to the ministry of someone whose lifestyle you can't respect.

Finally, "the God of peace shall be with you" (Phil. 4:9), said Paul, who ended on this note because he was addressing the issue of spiritual stability in the midst of trials. It takes us full circle to our original point of avoiding anxiety through prayer. When we follow that practice, "the peace of God, which surpasses all comprehension, shall guard [our] hearts and ... minds in Christ Jesus" (v. 7). There's no better protection from worry than that.

# 3

# CASTING YOUR
# CARES ON GOD

C⸙

T he apostle Peter was a worrier. He worried about drowning when he was walking on water, even though Jesus was right there with him (Matt. 14:29–31). He worried about what was going to happen to Jesus in the garden of Gethsemane, so he pulled out his sword and tried to take on a battalion of Roman soldiers (John 18:2–3, 10)—worry is never smart! For example, when Peter worried about Jesus being crucified, he *ordered* Jesus—God Almighty—not to go to the cross (Matt. 16:22). That took some guts! Nevertheless, although Peter had ongoing trouble with anxiety, he learned how to deal with it. He passed this lesson on to us:

> Clothe yourselves with humility toward one
> another, for God is opposed to the proud, but

gives grace to the humble. Humble yourselves, therefore, under the mighty hand of God, that He may exalt you at the proper time, casting all your anxiety upon Him, because He cares for you. (1 Peter 5:5–7)

To establish the context for you, verses 5–14 are the final section of Peter's first epistle. It could well be titled "Fundamental Attitudes for Spiritual Maturity." I think every sincere Christian thinks to himself or herself, *I want to be spiritually mature. I want to be spiritually effective. I want to be all that God wants me to be.* It's good to have those desires, but the reality comes to pass only when you and I build our lives on certain fundamentals. The one we will focus on is humility, for only from humility comes the ability to truly hand over all our cares to God.

## DEVELOP A HUMBLE ATTITUDE

Did you know that God has created a certain garment where one size fits everybody? When I was in New Orleans, I vividly recall an aggressive saleswoman who wouldn't leave me alone. She practically dragged me into her store, saying, "Why don't you come in? You might want to *buy* something." As I looked around, I observed that the only thing she sold was women's clothing. I said, "I have a basic rule: I don't buy women's clothes for me, and I don't buy women's clothes for my wife because I might get the wrong thing, especially since I'm out of town." She had a quick comeback: "Well, it doesn't matter. All these clothes fit everybody." I thought to myself, *If I brought home something for my wife that could fit everybody, she wouldn't take it as a compliment!* Only one garment can be honestly advertised as one size fits all, and that is the garment of humility, which every believer is commanded to put on.

## HUMILITY TOWARD OTHERS

When Peter said "clothe yourselves with humility toward one another" (1 Peter 5:5), he had a specific image in mind. He used a Greek term that means to tie something on yourself with a knot or a bow. It came to refer especially to a work apron. A slave would put on an apron over his or her clothes to keep them clean, just like you might do before you start a messy chore. The word became a synonym for humble service.

Humility is the attitude that you are not too good to serve others and that you are not too great to handle tasks that seem below you. Humility was not considered a virtue in the ancient world. Sadly, we have reverted to those times in this regard. Humble people today get mocked and trampled on. The world calls them wimps and instead exalts the proud. Although it was no different in Peter's day, he called us to be different.

In instructing us to put on the garment of a slave and serve others, Peter might have been thinking about his Lord. Recall the incident recorded in John 13, where Jesus "rose from supper, and laid aside His garments; and taking a towel, girded Himself about. Then He poured water into the basin, and began to wash the disciples' feet, and to wipe them with the towel with which He was girded" (vv. 4–5).

Here's the scene: The disciples were about to start supper with dirty feet. That was a problem because in the ancient Near East, people ate while reclining on floor mats. In a good-sized group, one person's head could be near another person's feet. It became customary for the lowliest person in the household to wash everyone's feet before they served the food.

Since none of the disciples volunteered to take on this servant role, Jesus took on the task Himself, leaving us all with an example of humble service. We clothe ourselves with humility toward one another when we meet each other's needs without regarding any task as being beneath us. Don't wait for someone else to step in and do the dirty work.

Another instructive text is Philippians 2:3–5:

> Do nothing from selfishness or empty conceit,
> but with humility of mind let each of you
> regard one another as more important than
> himself; do not merely look out for your own
> personal interests, but also for the interests of
> others. Have this attitude in yourselves which
> was also in Christ Jesus.

Be warned: It's a challenge to regard someone else as more important than yourself. Pride and selfishness dwell naturally within fallen human flesh. Jesus again is our example to follow. Paul went on to say how Christ at first existed in an exalted state with the Father, but then humbled Himself even to the point of a shameful death that He might serve us (vv. 6–8). The first step to enjoying the blessings of humility is to stoop to serve even the unworthy.

## HUMILITY TOWARD GOD

To support his exhortation to clothe ourselves in humility toward one another, Peter gave this citation from the Old Testament: "God is opposed to the proud, but gives grace to the humble" (1 Peter 5:5; cf. Prov. 3:34 NIV). That verse provides keen motivation for displaying humility. We will be blessed if we are humble and chastised if we are not. As we will soon see, one of those blessings is the ability to deal with anxiety.

First, however, let's explore why God is opposed to the proud. Very simply, He hates pride. According to Proverbs 6:16, "There are six things which the LORD hates, yes, seven which are an abomination to Him." What is first on the list? "Haughty eyes" (v. 17), a visual depiction of pride. A few chapters later, wisdom personified declares, "The fear of the LORD is to hate evil; pride and arrogance and the evil way, and the perverted mouth, I hate" (8:13).

God has a strong reason for hating pride so much; it is the sin that led to the fall of humanity, and it was the fatal flaw of the tempter who brought about such destruction. Pride is what prompted Lucifer to say in his heart:

I will ascend to heaven;
I will raise my throne above the stars of God,
And I will sit on the mount of assembly
In the recesses of the north.
I will ascend above the heights of the clouds;
I will make myself like the Most High.
(Isa. 14:13–14)

God's grace is reserved for the humble.

For thus says the high and exalted One who lives
forever, whose name is Holy, "I dwell on a high
and holy place, and also with the contrite and lowly
of spirit in order to revive the spirit of the lowly
and to revive the heart of the contrite." (57:15)

God lives in an exalted place. Who lives with Him there? Not the high and mighty, but the lowly.

God concluded His message to Isaiah by saying, "To this one I will look, to him who is humble and contrite of spirit, and who trembles at My word" (66:2). He blesses the humble, but He opposes the proud. I mourn to see people stumbling around trying to fix their lives, to find some kind of solution, some kind of book or therapy that will solve their problems, but who find no deliverance. Instead of experiencing the grace of God, they experience the correcting hand of God because they are proud.

Peter's advice is, "Humble yourselves, therefore, under the mighty hand of God, that He may exalt you at the proper time" (1 Peter 5:6). After all, "He has told you, O man, what is good; and what does the LORD require of you but to do justice, to love kindness, and to walk humbly with your God?" (Mic. 6:8). The key is never to contest God's wisdom, but instead to accept humbly whatever God brings into your life as coming from His hand.

"The mighty hand of God" is an Old Testament symbol of God's controlling power. The humble person realizes that God is in charge, always accomplishing His sovereign purposes. That realization, however, should not go so far as to produce the fatalistic attitude of crying uncle to God—like, "God, You're too strong for me to contend with. No use battering my head against the walls of the universe." For over eight hundred years, perhaps no one has portrayed that attitude more wrenchingly than Omar Khayyám in *The Rubaiyat*:

> But helpless Pieces of the Game He plays
> Upon this Chequer-board of Nights and Days;
> Hither and thither moves, and checks, and slays,

And one by one back in the Closet lays.

The Ball no question makes of Ayes and Noes,
But Here or There as strikes the Player goes;
And He that toss'd you down into the Field,
He knows about it all—He knows—HE knows!

The Moving Finger writes; and, having writ,
Moves on: nor all your Piety nor Wit
Shall lure it back to cancel half a Line,
Nor all your Tears wash out a Word of it.
(stanzas LXIX–LXXI)


Yes, God is all-powerful. Contrary to the fanciful characters of some science-fiction shows, He is the *only* omnipotent being. He is capable of doing all Khayyám wrote about and more, but the balancing factor is that God cares about us. We will soon explore that truth in more detail.

In Scripture the mighty hand of God's power means different things at different times. Sometimes it speaks of deliverance, as in the exodus of Israel from Egypt (Ex. 3:20). Sometimes it serves as a shield to protect the believer through a time of testing. Sometimes it is a chastening hand.

Let's look at a specific example from the book of Job. In the midst of terrible suffering, Job tragically compounded his anguish by doing what he should have learned never to do: He contested God's wisdom, expressly resenting what the mighty hand of God had brought him. Take time to sense the raw human emotion seething under the words of his lament:

I cry out to you, O God, but you do not
answer; I stand up, but you merely look at me.
You turn on me ruthlessly; with the might of

your hand you attack me. You snatch me up and drive me before the wind; you toss me about in the storm. I know you will bring me down to death. (30:20–23 NIV)

Perhaps Job was feeling like one of Khayyám's chess pieces. Here the mighty hand of God is not the hand of deliverance but of testing, acting like the refiner's fire to make Job's faith come out like gold. Contrary to Job's gloomy expectations, that's exactly what happened. Once God had humbled him, Job confessed, "Surely I spoke of things I did not understand, things too wonderful for me to know.... My ears had heard of you but now my eyes have seen you. Therefore I despise myself and repent in dust and ashes" (42:3, 5–6 NIV). Job was saying, "God, now I see You like never before! I have learned that my perceptions are seriously limited, but now I know I can trust You implicitly."

Job's example is recorded for us, so we can learn the same lesson without having to go through the same struggles. Paul said, "Whatever was written in earlier times was written for our instruction, that through perseverance and the encouragement of the Scriptures we might have hope" (Rom. 15:4). Never view the mighty hand of God in your life as a slap in the face but as grounds for hope. Realize He has only good intentions toward you as His child, and therefore expect to see good results from your present circumstances. Such an attitude leaves no steam for worry to operate on.

Peter said when you humble yourself under God's mighty hand, "He may exalt you at the proper time" (1 Peter 5:6). What's the proper time? His time, not our time. When will it be? When He has accomplished His purpose. Now that might seem a little vague, but there's no cause for concern: God has perfect timing. Indeed, our salvation depended on His perfect timing. Paul specified that the hope of eternal life was "at the proper time manifested" through Jesus Christ (Titus 1:2–3). Trusting in God's timing is no light or peripheral matter to the Christian faith.

At the proper time God will exalt us. Paul used a Greek term that speaks of lifting us out of our present trouble. For the Christian, even the worst trial is only temporary. *Remember that,* for you *will* be tempted to conclude that because there's no end in sight, there is no end at all. Don't believe it for a minute; God promises to lift you out.[1]

How are we to conduct ourselves until the promised time of deliverance? Peter said, "Humble yourselves … casting all your anxiety upon Him, because He cares for you" (1 Peter 5:6–7).

## LEARN TO TRUST

Humility requires strong confidence in a caring God. I can't humble myself under God's pressure if I don't think He cares, but I can if I know He does. Peter said to have an attitude of trust. The basis of that trust is the loving care God has repeatedly shown us. You cast your anxiety on Him when you're able to say, however haltingly, "Lord, it's difficult … I'm having trouble handling this trial, but I'm giving You the whole deal because I know You care for me."

The word translated "casting" was used to describe throwing something on something else, such as a blanket over a pack animal (e.g., Luke 19:35). Take all your anxiety—all the discontent, discouragement, despair, questioning, pain, and suffering that you're going through—and toss it all onto God. Trade it in for trust in God, who really cares about you.

Hannah is a great illustration of someone who did just that. She didn't have any children, which was a significant trial for a Jewish woman in ancient times. The book of 1 Samuel tells us what she did about her problem:

> She, greatly distressed, prayed to the LORD and wept bitterly. And she made a vow and said, "O LORD of hosts, if Thou wilt indeed look on the affliction of Thy maidservant and remember me, and not forget Thy maidservant, but wilt give Thy maidservant a son, then I will give him to the LORD all the days of his life...."
>
> Now it came about, as she continued praying before the LORD, that Eli [the priest] was watching her mouth. As for Hannah, she was speaking in her heart, only her lips were moving, but her voice was not heard. So Eli thought she was drunk. Then Eli said to her, "How long will you make yourself drunk? Put away your wine from you." But Hannah answered and said, "No, my lord, I am a woman oppressed in spirit; I have drunk neither wine nor strong drink, but I have poured out my soul before the Lord. Do not consider your maidservant as a worthless woman; for I have spoken until now out of my great concern and provocation." Then Eli answered and said, "Go in peace; and may the God of Israel grant your petition that you have asked of Him." And she said, "Let your maidservant find favor in your sight." So the woman went her way and ate, and her face was no longer sad. (1:10–18)

What happened to her? Why was she no longer sad? Her circumstances hadn't changed, but *she changed* when she cast her care on the Lord. Soon thereafter, God blessed her with a son, Samuel, who grew to be a great man of God. God also gave her three other sons and two daughters. Hannah is proof: When you remain humble under the mighty hand of God, giving Him all your anxiety on His loving care, He will exalt you in due time.

There's no doubt in my mind that Peter had Psalm 55:22 in mind when he wrote his first epistle: "Cast your burden upon the LORD, and He will sustain you; He will never allow the righteous to be shaken." Now that doesn't mean we won't feel shaky at times. Think how Hannah felt when the priest accused her of being drunk. Sometimes when we're bearing burdens that in themselves seem too great to bear, people treat us insensitively and heap more burdens on us. But, like Hannah, we can be gracious about it and find relief through prayer to the God who does care.

If you need to be reminded now and then that God really cares about you, remember what Jesus said in the Sermon on the Mount: Since He luxuriously arrays mere field lilies, don't you think He will clothe you? Since He faithfully feeds mere birds, don't you think He will feed you? Spiritual maturity begins with these fundamentals: an attitude of humility toward God and others and trust in God's care.

What will that attitude of trust look like when dealing with fear and anxiety? We go again to Jay Adams for some practical advice:

> Stop trying to stop fearing [or worrying].
> Say to God in your own words (and mean it)
> something like this: "Lord, if I have another

[bout with fear or worry], I'll just have to have it. I am going to leave that in your hands." That is something of what Peter meant when he wrote: "Casting all of your care upon Him for He cares for you" (1 Peter 5:7). Then, make your plans and go ahead and do whatever God holds you responsible for doing. Fill your mind with concern for the other persons toward whom you are expressing love and how you will do so, in whatever you are doing.[2]

A prayer found in a small devotional manual that first appeared in Europe over five hundred years ago prepares us to follow through with that advice. The manual is attributed to Thomas à Kempis and is titled *The Imitation of Christ:*

O Lord ... greater is Thy anxiety for me (Matt. 6:30; John 6:20), than all the care that I can take for myself. For he standeth but very totteringly, who casteth not all his anxiety upon Thee. (1 Peter 5:7)

O Lord, if only my will may remain right and firm towards Thee, do with me whatsoever it shall please Thee. For it cannot be anything but good, whatsoever Thou shalt do with me. If Thou willest me to be in darkness, be Thou blessed; and if Thou willest me to be in light, be Thou again blessed. If Thou vouchsafe to comfort me, be Thou blessed; and if Thou willest me to be afflicted, be Thou ever equally blessed.[3]

# LIVING A LIFE OF
# FAITH AND TRUST

ℭℐ

Ge  orge Müller knew a lot about faith—the best way anyone can know anything: He lived by it. His early life was one
of gross wickedness. By the time he was twenty, the age he
became a Christian, he had already done time in jail. But
then his interests and attitude radically changed.

After Müller spent years training for the ministry, he went
to England to do missionary work among Jewish people.
When he and his wife moved to the British seaport of Bristol
in 1832, they were horrified to see masses of homeless orphans
living and dying in squalid, narrow streets and foraging for
food in garbage heaps.

The Müllers, with an unshakable belief in the Bible, were
convinced that if Christians took Scripture seriously, there
were no limits to what they could achieve for God. They set

out to feed, clothe, and educate destitute orphan children. At the end of the Müllers' lifetimes, the homes they established cared for more than ten thousand orphans. Unlike many today who say they "live by faith," the Müllers never told anyone but God of their need for funds. He always abundantly provided through their thankful prayers and humble waiting on Him.

George Müller said, "Where faith begins, anxiety ends; where anxiety begins, faith ends."[1] Because of his exemplary life, we can believe he knew what he was talking about. If we would do a comprehensive study on what Scripture says about anxiety, we would need to examine what it says about living by faith.

Hebrews 11 and 12 are the faith chapters of the Bible. Chapter 11 gives a general definition of faith and a slew of Old Testament examples. As we noted about Job in our previous chapter, God supplied us with examples from the past so we might be encouraged and have hope when we see how these very real people were able to handle their anxieties. Chapter 12 of Hebrews sums up the principles of living by faith. As we will see, there's much more to it than the contemporary sense that limits it to handling one's personal finances.

## LAY ASIDE ANY ENCUMBRANCE

The writer of Hebrews said to "lay aside every encumbrance, and the sin which so easily entangles us, and let us run with endurance the race that is set before us" (12:1). When you first learn to run, you quickly find out that you have to run light. You may train in a sweat suit with weights strapped on, but you need to take them off before you get to the starting blocks. The effective runner gets rid of the bulk and runs with the bare minimum.

Similarly, in the race of faith we need to strip off anything that will hold us back. Many things can weigh us down and hold us back in the Christian life: Materialism, sexual immorality, and excessive ambition are just a few that are common in our society. One of the things the writer of Hebrews probably had in mind was legalism. He was writing to a predominantly Jewish audience that struggled with that issue. They were trying to run the race with all their Jewish ceremonies, rituals, and rites. In essence, this writer said, "Get rid of all of that and run the race of faith. Live by faith, not works."

Many Christians still live by works. They believe if they do certain things, God is obliged to keep score and say, "That's wonderful: You went to a Bible study, had a quiet time in the Word today, did something nice for your neighbor, and went to church." If those things are done in the overflow of one's love for Jesus Christ as acts of devotion, that's great. But there are many Christians who think they are meriting God's favor that way. Instead of Jewish legalism, it's Christian legalism.

Another weight or sin that "so easily entangles us" is doubt. A believer may strongly sense in his or her heart the truth of Philippians 4:19—"God shall supply all your needs according to His riches in glory in Christ Jesus"—but become filled with anxiety when financial trouble comes. Then others will inevitably say, "Aren't you the one who goes around saying, 'God shall supply all your needs'?" We either believe He will or He won't, regardless of what we say. Our actions reveal what we really believe. When we worry, we are doubting that God can keep His promises, and that dishonors Him.

The Bible also points out that if we give sacrificially with the proper motives, God will reward us (Matt. 6:3–4). We say we believe that principle as well, but we often find it difficult to put it into practice. To be honest, most of us need to admit that we don't believe God as much as we claim.

What is our protection against doubt? Paul said that above all, take "up the shield of faith with which you will be able to extinguish all the flaming missiles of the evil one" (Eph. 6:16). When Satan fires his temptations, we stop them with the shield of faith. It's arming ourselves with an attitude that says, "Satan, you're a big liar. Nothing you say is true, but everything God says is true, so I'm going to believe God."

Every time we sin, it's because we believe Satan instead of God. That is why the writer of Hebrews wanted believers to get rid of their doubts and anything else that hinders them and run this race with confidence, realizing that they have excellent examples who lived the same life of faith, ran the same race, and were triumphant.

## LOOK TO JESUS

The writer of Hebrews also said we're to be "fixing our eyes on Jesus the author and perfecter of faith, who for the joy set before Him endured the cross, despising the shame, and has sat down at the right hand of the throne of God" (Heb. 12:2). Jesus is the greatest example of faith who ever lived because He had the most to lose.

Paul explained further, "Although [Jesus] existed in the form of God, [He] did not regard equality with God a thing to be grasped, but emptied Himself, taking the form of a bond-servant, and being made in the likeness of men. And being found in appearance as a man, He humbled Himself by becoming obedient to the point of death, even death on a cross" (Phil. 2:6–8). Our Lord set aside His divine rights and believed God, who said He would not let His Holy One see corruption (Ps. 16:10). He came into the world as a man, bore the sins of the world, and died in the confidence that He would be raised by the Father and exalted once again. His act of faith remains forever unsurpassed. Our Lord Jesus Christ endured unimaginable suffering, but in believing God, He was victorious. That is why we're to focus on Him.

The phrase "fixing our eyes on Jesus" is literally translated "looking away to Jesus." Having the right focus is essential to completing any goal successfully. When my dad was teaching me how to hit a baseball, he'd say, "You can't hit a baseball unless you keep your eye on it as it's coming toward you." When we played basketball, he'd say, "Keep your eye on the basket."

Similarly, in the Christian life your focal point must be beyond yourself. In fact, the sooner you get your eyes off yourself the better off you will be. I see much harm coming from the current preoccupation with psychotherapy and intensive introspection. We can get so wrapped up watching ourselves that it's like trying to drive a car while watching the pedals.

When you run in a race, you shouldn't look at your feet. You shouldn't even look too intently at the other runners—just at Jesus. He's the perfect example, "the author and perfecter of faith." The Greek word translated "author" is *archēgos* and means originator, pioneer, primogenitor, and supreme leader. Christ is the chief leader of faith, greater than any example in Hebrews 11—or anywhere else. He provides a balance to those who might otherwise compare themselves too readily with other believers and jealously desire their faith or experiences.

What awaits us at the finish line of the race of faith? Joy and triumph. Jesus endured the cross "for the joy set before

Him" (Heb. 12:2). Any athlete will tell you that there's nothing equal to the thrill of winning. It isn't the medal or trophy or anything else—it's just the winning, the exhilaration of victory. For Jesus it was the joy of again being seated "at the right hand of the throne of God" (v. 2).

Ultimately, our real joy and reward as believers is to be in heaven with Christ, but here and now we can experience a great sense of triumph when we have victory over temptation. As you know, there are plenty of temptations to face. Here are some familiar voices, perhaps one being your own: "It's not easy being a Christian. I'm ridiculed at work.... They short me on my office supplies.... My philosophy teacher attacks my beliefs in class.... My spouse makes our home life difficult.... It's getting harder and harder to be a Christian in our society because we're getting close to the end times."

On that last point, more than ever I hear believers say, "We're worried about what's happening in the world. If things don't change in our country real fast, we're finished." Christians shouldn't live that way. We don't live by the news; we live by faith in God.

When Bulstrode Whitelock was preparing to embark as Oliver Cromwell's envoy to Sweden in 1653, he was feeling anxious about the tumultuous state of his nation. England had recently gone through civil war, and—for the first and only time in its history—it executed its own king (Charles I). The army and the government were at odds with each other. So were the Presbyterians and Cromwell's Independents, two branches of Puritans (spiritual heirs of the Reformers from the previous century). It was difficult enough figuring out which direction the country was headed, let alone representing it to another country. The night before his journey, Whitelock nervously paced about. A trusted servant, noticing his employer was unable to sleep, approached him after a while. This exchange took place:

> "Pray, sir, will you give me leave to ask you a question?"
>
> "Certainly."
>
> "Pray, sir, do you not think that God governed the world very well before you came into it?"
>
> "Undoubtedly."
>
> "And pray, sir, do you not think that He will govern it quite as well when you are gone out of it?"
>
> "Certainly."
>
> "Then, sir, pray excuse me, but do not you think you may trust Him to govern it quite as well as long as you live?"[2]

The question left Whitelock speechless. He headed for bed and soon was fast asleep. Similarly, we do well to ask ourselves those same questions when fearing what will happen to us in today's world, then rest easy when realizing the obvious answer.

The author of Hebrews was keenly aware that many such concerns in running the Christian marathon would plague us. Therefore, this is what he said to do: "Consider Him who has endured such hostility by sinners against Himself, so that you may not grow weary and lose heart. You have not yet resisted to the point of shedding blood, in your striving against sin" (12:3–4). In other words, "I don't see any of you bleeding. It may be a little rough at work, you may get hassled in class, and you probably won't get preferential treatment by the government or anyone else, but you haven't been crucified like Someone I know."

When you start thinking it's too tough to live the Christian life, consider One who endured such hostility that He went as far as death—and realize you haven't gone that far yet. Having that in mind has a way of keeping your anxieties in check. When you grow weary in the race, focus that much more on Jesus. Remember that His life of faith led to joy and triumph, and yours will too.

## PRAISE GOD NOW

As I mentioned earlier, the Christian's joy isn't relegated only to the future. A great part of our future will be devoted to joyfully praising God, and that's something we can begin doing now. Proud people don't praise God; they're too consumed with themselves. Humble people are in awe of Him; thankful praise pours naturally from their hearts. In the last two chapters, we chronicled from God's Word the benefits of humility and thankful prayer in getting rid of anxiety. Here we see the two join as one in praise—an awesome weapon in our growing arsenal for attacking anxious thoughts and feelings.

### THE EXAMPLE OF THE PSALMS

Only half facetiously did I once suggest to my congregation that any Christian paralyzed by anxiety should be sequestered to a simply furnished room, given food through a slot in the door, and not let out until he or she had read the book of Psalms! Those undergoing this "psalm therapy" would know so much about God that they couldn't help but praise Him. The point, as the author of Hebrews would say, is to get our focus off ourselves and onto God. Anxiety cannot survive in an environment of praise to God.

Praise is so much a part of God's pattern for His people that He left us with a hymnbook filled with it. The Psalms are great hymns that the people of Israel sang and spoke. God wanted them—and us—to continually offer Him the praise of which He is so worthy. "It is good to give thanks to the LORD, and to sing praises to Thy name, O Most High; to declare Thy lovingkindness in the morning, and Thy faithfulness by night" (Ps. 92:1–2). Praising the Lord morning and night sets the tone for our lives.

## ASPECTS OF PRAISE

What exactly does it mean to praise God? Some think it is singing a song. Some think it is saying, "Praise the Lord! Hallelujah!" Some think it is waving your hands in the air. Some think it is silent prayer. What is the right answer? How do we praise the Lord? According to the Bible, true praise involves two things.

### Reciting God's attributes

Praise expresses the character of God. Some Christians study the New Testament almost exclusively because it reveals many truths that were mysteries in the past. But one great reason to study the Old Testament is that it powerfully reveals the character of God, enabling us to praise Him better.

For example, Habakkuk praised God for His character—that He is a holy, almighty, eternal, covenant-keeping God (Hab. 1:12–13)—and that praise solved a great problem in his own heart. He didn't understand why God was going to judge Israel by sending the evil Chaldeans to conquer them (vv. 6–11). Habakkuk wanted God to revive and restore His people, but they had overstepped the limit of His patience.

In the midst of his confusion, Habakkuk remembered this: God is holy—He doesn't make mistakes. God is a covenant-keeping God—He doesn't break His promises. God is eternal—He is outside the flux of history. Following his praise, Habakkuk affirmed what we have been learning throughout this chapter, that "the righteous will live by his faith" (2:4).

He felt better even though his circumstances hadn't changed. God did allow the Chaldeans to overrun Israel for a time, but Habakkuk knew his God was strong enough to handle any circumstances.

Instead of worrying about problems we cannot solve, we should say, "Lord, You are bigger than history. You own everything in the entire universe. You can do anything You want to do. You love me and promise I will never be without the things I need. You said You would take care of me as You take care of the birds and the flowers. You have promised that Your character and power are at my disposal." That kind of praise glorifies God.

### Reciting God's works

God's attributes are displayed in His works. The Psalms are filled with lists of the great things God has done for His people. They praise Him for parting the Red Sea, making water flow from a rock, feeding His people with manna in the wilderness, destroying their enemies, making the walls of Jericho fall, and many other powerful works.

After reevaluating his problem, Habakkuk began to praise God for His works, trembling at the power displayed in them

(3:16). He affirmed that he would rejoice in the Lord even if everything crumbled about him (vv. 17–18). Why? Because God had proved Himself in the past. That's why the Old Testament contains such an extensive history of God's works—so we can know specifically *how* God has proved faithful.

If you have a problem facing you that you don't know how to solve, remember to praise God. Say to Him, "Lord, You are the God who put the stars and planets into space. You are the God who formed the earth and separated the land from the sea. Then You made humanity and everything else that lives. Although humanity fell, You planned our redemption. You are the God who carved out a nation for Yourself and preserved it through history, performing wonder after wonder for that nation. You are the God who came into this world in human form and then rose from the dead." When we praise God like that, our problems pale in comparison to all He has done.

Remembering who God is and what He has done glorifies Him and strengthens our faith. To help you do that, read through the Psalms the next time you're tempted to worry. Although I really was joking about forcing anxious Christians to do that, I am so serious about the blessing they will be to your life that I present you with an appendix at the end of this book titled "Psalms for the Anxious." It is an abridged collection of psalms, offering those portions that most poignantly express and help us manage our anxious thoughts and feelings. Perhaps you'll want to lock *yourself* in a room to study them. Then it will quickly become evident to you how they can help you have greater faith and trust in God!

# 5

# Knowing Others Are Looking Out for You

ॐ

Until now, we have been examining one specific biblical passage per chapter, which is the best way of first knowing and then applying Scripture to our own lives. Here, however, we will focus on how *others* help us in our personal war against anxiety. I trust it will be a helpful reminder that the Christian life was never meant to be a solitary struggle.

The extensive support system of Christian fellowship is one of the greatest benefits of being a Christian. We are all part of a loving family that takes care of one another. We will soon explore how the Bible says we're to do that, and how that relates to anxiety, but first consider what it says about a nameless group of individuals who help us more each day than we can possibly know. I am referring to angels, whom the writer of Hebrews 1:14 described as "ministering spirits, sent out to render service for the sake of those who will inherit salvation." Since we are the heirs of salvation, God sends His angels to minister to us.

## ANGELS WATCHING OVER YOU

Perhaps the word *minister* seems a little stuffy to you, or perhaps it reminds you of a stuffy individual! It really is a practical term. C. S. Lewis illustrated that well in his children's classic *The Lion, the Witch and the Wardrobe* from The Chronicles of Narnia series. Three children, after an arduous journey through the winter-cursed regions ruled by the White Witch, finally reach the royal retinue of Aslan, the mighty Christlike lion. Aslan takes aside the young boy to speak with him, but before he does, he shakes his mane, claps his immense yet velvety paws together, and orders, "Ladies, take these Daughters of Eve to the pavilion and minister to them."[1] The weary travelers received refreshment, and so do we at the hands of those who minister to us in our life's journey.

A while ago my church and I embarked on a study of God, Satan, and angels. What strongly impressed me at the time are the steps God has taken to make His children physically secure through the ministry of angels. It is a lesson that has stayed with me. God details in His Word how angels aid us and therefore help many of the anxieties we tend to have about accidents, disease, or other kinds of danger. We see on display God's tremendous sovereign control over the world and universe through His creative power, which includes angelic beings.

In his book *Angels: God's Secret Agents,* Billy Graham's attitude reflects a healthy perspective we should have when we study about angels:

I am convinced that these heavenly beings exist
and that they provide unseen aid on our behalf.
I do not believe in angels because someone has
told me about a dramatic visitation from an
angel, impressive as such rare testimonies may
be. I do not believe in angels because UFO's
are astonishingly angel-like in some of their
reported appearances. I do not believe in angels
because ESP experts are making the realm of
the spirit world seem more and more plausible.
I do not believe in angels because of the sud-
den worldwide emphasis on the reality of Satan
and demons. I do not believe in angels because
I have ever seen one—because I haven't. I
believe in angels because the Bible says there
are angels; and I believe the Bible to be the
true Word of God.[2]

Some of the many things angels do on our behalf are
guiding, providing, protecting, delivering, facilitating, and
serving.

## GUIDING

The Holy Spirit guides the believer internally, while the
angels guide the believer externally.

As the evangelist Philip preached to large crowds in
Samaria, "an angel of the Lord spoke to [him] saying, 'Arise
and go south to the road that descends from Jerusalem to
Gaza.' ... And he arose and went; and behold, there was an
Ethiopian eunuch, a court official of Candace, queen of the
Ethiopians, who was in charge of all her treasure; and he had

come to Jerusalem to worship" (Acts 8:26–27). Philip had a wonderful conversation with him and led him to Christ (vv. 29–39). The angel guided Philip out of one ministry into another. Angels do the same for us today.

### PROVIDING

When the prophet Elijah heard that the evil Queen Jezebel was out to get him because the pagan priests in her service were slain, he panicked and ran out of town (1 Kings 19:1–3).

> [Elijah] went a day's journey into the wilderness, and came and sat down under a juniper tree; and he requested for himself that he might die, and said, "It is enough; now, O Lord, take my life...." And he lay down and slept under a juniper tree; and behold, there was an angel touching him, and he said to him, "Arise, eat." Then he looked and behold, there was at his head a bread cake baked on hot stones, and a jar of water. So he ate and drank and lay down again. And the angel of the Lord came again a second time and touched him and said, "Arise, eat, because the journey is too great for you." So he arose and ate and drank, and went in the strength of that food forty days and forty nights. (vv. 4–8)

An angel provided sustenance for the physically and emotionally exhausted prophet. That's comforting to know when we're feeling as bad as Elijah felt. It's possible angels have ministered the same way to us without our knowing it. Hebrews 13:2 says that "some have entertained angels without knowing it," and perhaps they have returned the favor.

## PROTECTING

Angels also protect God's people from physical danger. Two of the most dramatic examples are from the book of Daniel, in which an angel protected Daniel's three friends Shadrach, Meshach, and Abednego from burning in a fiery furnace and Daniel from being attacked in a lions' den (Dan. 3:28; 6:22).

There's another fascinating example from the New Testament. As the apostle Paul sailed across the Mediterranean Sea to stand trial in Rome, his ship was caught in a storm so violent that the crew "began to jettison the cargo; and on the third day they threw the ship's tackle overboard with their own hands. And since neither sun nor stars appeared for many days, and no small storm was assailing [them], from then on all hope of [their] being saved was gradually abandoned" (Acts 27:18–20).

It was a good time for angelic intervention. "When they had gone a long time without food, then Paul stood up in their midst and said, 'Men, ... I urge you to keep up your courage, for there shall be no loss of life among you, but only of the ship. For this very night an angel of the God to whom I belong and whom I serve stood before me, saying, "Do not be afraid, Paul; you must stand before Caesar; and behold, God has granted you all those who are sailing with you"'" (vv. 21–24). While that ship was being battered about on the Mediterranean, there might have been a legion of angels protecting everyone on board. In fact, the sea destroyed the ship, yet everyone made it safely to shore. It happened just as the angel said it would.

God's angels protect His people, and sometimes these angels graciously spare others in their midst who don't acknowledge Jesus as their Lord and Savior. Angels take care of us when we drive on the highway, and they protect our children. Since I know God has His angels looking out for my children, I don't worry about them because angels can do things for them that I couldn't even if I were with them.

## DELIVERING

This word doesn't refer to preventing trouble, but to getting people out of trouble. In its infancy the church experienced tremendous growth because of the apostles' preaching. Since the religious leaders of Israel felt threatened by the church's popularity, they decided to imprison the apostles.

> But an angel of the Lord by night opened the prison doors, and brought them forth, and said, Go, stand and speak in the temple to the people all the words of this life. And when they heard that, they entered into the temple early in the morning, and taught....
>
> When the officers came, and found them not in the prison, they returned, and told, saying, The prison truly found we shut with all safety, and the keepers standing without before the doors; but when we had opened, we found no man within. (Acts 5:19–23 SCO)

How did they get out? The angel let them out. It's exciting to know you can't ever get yourself into a situation that God can't remove you from if He so chooses. Let that truth help melt away any anxieties you have about a situation you currently dread.

The persecution of the early church intensified quickly. James was executed, and Peter was thrown into prison (12:2–4). On the night he was to be executed:

> Peter was sleeping between two soldiers, bound with two chains; and the keepers before the door kept the prison. And, behold, an angel of the Lord came upon him, and a light shone in the prison; and he smote Peter on the side, and raised him up, saying, Arise quickly. And his chains fell off from his hands. And the angel said unto him, Gird thyself, and bind on thy sandals. And so he did. And he saith unto him, Cast thy garment about thee, and follow me. And he went out, and followed him; and knew not that it was true which was done by the angel, but thought he saw a vision. When they were past the first and the second guard, they came unto the iron gate that leadeth unto the city, which opened to them of its own accord; and they went out, and passed on through one street; and immediately the angel departed from him. And when Peter was come to himself, he said, Now I know of a surety that the Lord hath sent his angel, and hath delivered me. (vv. 6–11 sco)

Think how active God and His angels must have been in the lives of all the people referred to in Hebrews 11. They delivered Gideon, Barak, Samson, Jephthah, David, Samuel, and the prophets, "who, through faith, subdued kingdoms, wrought righteousness, obtained promises, stopped the mouths of lions, quenched the violence of fire, escaped the edge of the sword" (vv. 33–34 SCO). Throughout history, angels have served God's people by protecting and delivering them. That includes contemporary history.

## FACILITATING

Angels do not answer prayer themselves but can be involved in facilitating God's answers to prayer. The angel who took Peter out of prison did so in response to the fervent prayers of the church (Acts 12:5): God sent the angel to deliver Peter in answer to their prayers. In Daniel 9 and 10, there are other examples of God sending an angel in answer to prayer.

## SERVING

During the millennial kingdom, angels will serve us as we rule. Paul said, "Do you not know that the saints will judge the world? ... Do you not know that we shall judge [rule over] angels?" (1 Cor. 6:2–3). In the coming kingdom we will rule on earth with Christ as co-regents and joint heirs (Rev. 20:4; Matt. 19:28; Rom. 8:17). The angels will be subject to us.

What should be our attitude toward angels? We ought to respect them as holy servants of God. We ought to appreciate them, knowing how they help us through our difficulties. And we ought to follow their example of continual worship and service to God.

## FELLOW BELIEVERS AT YOUR SERVICE

One of the best ways we can be helped in our struggle with anxiety is when we serve one another with the same diligence as the angels serve us. Does that sound impossible? It's not. The same God who equips the angels to serve us also equips us to serve one another. Paul said, "There are diversities of gifts, but the same Spirit. And there are differences of administrations, but the same Lord. And there are diversities of operations, but it is the same God who worketh all in all" (1 Cor. 12:4–6 SCO). God has given a variety of gifts to His church.

### USING OUR GIFTS

Some of the gifts were of a temporary nature; others were and are permanent. The temporary ones were miracles, healings, and tongues.[3] The permanent ones are these:

- Prophecy (Rom. 12:6; 1 Cor. 14:3), the ability to preach or proclaim God's truth to others for their growth, correction, and comfort.
- Teaching (Rom. 12:7), the ability to teach the truths of God's Word.
- Faith (1 Cor. 12:9), the ability to trust God without doubt or disturbance, regardless of one's circumstances. People who are especially prone to anxiety would do well to get to know individuals gifted in this way and follow their example.

- *Wisdom* (1 Cor. 12:8), the ability to apply spiritual truth to life. Believers gifted this way are also good models for the anxious.

- *Knowledge* (1 Cor. 12:8), the ability to understand facts. It is the academic side of comprehending biblical truth.

- *Discernment* (1 Cor. 12:10), the ability to distinguish truth from error—to discern what is of God and what is satanic deception.

- *Mercy* (Rom. 12:8), the ability to demonstrate Christ's love in acts of kindness.

- *Exhortation* (Rom. 12:8), the ability to encourage, counsel, and comfort others with biblical truth and Christian love. Those prone to anxiety need to be humble enough to listen and value what these gifted individuals have to say.

- *Giving* (Rom. 12:8), the ability to provide for the Lord's work and for others who have difficulty meeting their own material needs. It flows from a decision to commit all earthly possessions to the Lord.

- *Administration* (Rom. 12:8; 1 Cor. 12:28), the ability to organize and lead in spiritual endeavors. It is also known as the gift of ruling or government.

- *Helps* (Rom. 12:7; 1 Cor. 12:28), the ability to serve faithfully behind the scenes, assisting the work of the ministry in practical ways.

All spiritual gifts are designed for the good of the church (1 Cor. 14:26 NIV). My gifts are not for my benefit, and your gifts are not for your benefit. We must build up and assist one another "until we all attain to the unity of the faith, and of the knowledge of the Son of God, to a mature man, to the measure of the stature which belongs to the fullness of Christ" (Eph. 4:13).

Fellowship is an interchange of mutual care and concern through the agency of our spiritual gifts. Some of the ways that interchange manifests itself are when we:

- Confess our faults to one another (James 5:16).
- Edify one another (1 Thess. 5:11; Rom. 14:19).
- Bear one another's burdens (Gal. 6:2).
- Pray for one another (James 5:16).
- Are kind to one another (Eph. 4:32).
- Submit to one another (Eph. 5:21).
- Show hospitality to one another (1 Peter 4:9).
- Serve one another (Gal. 5:13; 1 Peter 4:10).
- Comfort one another (1 Thess. 4:18).
- Restore one another (Gal. 6:1).
- Forgive one another (2 Cor. 2:7; Eph. 4:32; Col. 3:13).
- Admonish one another (Rom. 15:14; Col. 3:16).
- Teach one another (Col. 3:16).
- Exhort one another (Heb. 3:13; 10:25).
- Love one another (Rom. 13:8; 1 Thess. 3:12; 4:9; 1 Peter 1:22; 1 John 3:11, 23; 4:7, 11).

Love is the key to effective ministry. Where love exists there is true humility, which is an essential ingredient in mutual ministries *and* freedom from anxiety. Pride and anxiety focus on self, whereas humility focuses on others.

If pride is hindering your ministry, concentrate on knowing Christ more intimately through prayer and Bible study. The more you understand His power and glory, the more humble you will be. Then you will give yourself more readily to others as Christ gave Himself to you.

### SHARING OUR LOVE

As a human body has connected tissues, muscles, bones, ligaments, and organs, the body of Christ is composed of members who are responsible to one another. No member exists detached from the rest of the body any more than lungs can lie on the floor in the next room and keep a person breathing. The health of the body, its witness, and its testimony are dependent on all members faithfully ministering to one another.

The church was never intended to be only a building—a place where lonely people walk in, listen, and walk out still alone—but a place of fellowship. In his book *Dare to Live Now!* Bruce Larson says:

> The neighborhood bar is possibly the best counterfeit there is to the fellowship Christ wants to give His Church. It's an imitation, dispensing liquor instead of grace, escape rather than reality. But it is a permissive, accepting, and inclusive fellowship. It is unshockable, it is democratic. You can tell people secrets and they

usually don't tell others, or want to. The bar
flourishes not because most people are alco-
holics, but because God has put into the human
heart the desire to know and be known, to love,
and be loved, and so many seek a counterfeit at
the price of a few beers.[4]

This need for fellowship is not met simply by attending the
Sunday services, whether they be small groups where everyone
is known or large congregations where that is not the case. A
desperate need for personal, intimate fellowship exists in the
church today. And this fellowship, like the gifts, is intrinsic to
exhibiting practical unity. Finding a good church fellowship is
no small matter in our onslaught against anxiety.

In true fellowship Christians don't judge one another; they
don't bite and devour each other; they don't provoke, envy, lie
to one another, speak evil, or grumble about one another. Since
true fellowship builds up, the godly will receive one another
and be kind and tenderhearted toward one another. They will
bear with and forgive one another, serve one another, practice
hospitality ungrudgingly to one another, correct, instruct, submit to one another, and comfort one another. That is the true
fellowship of Christ's body—life touching life to bring blessing
and spiritual growth.

Too often Christians place themselves inside little glass
bubbles and try to look like supersaints, as if they hadn't a
problem or worry in the world. They aren't willing to share
openly and expose their sins to a fellow believer. They don't
know what it is to have another believer say, "That's the same
thing I'm going through. Let's pray for each other."

A brother in Christ confessed a sin to me and promised
to tell me each time he committed it. Later he told me that

promise prevented him from committing the sin again because he didn't want to endure the shame of telling me about it. Dietrich Bonhoeffer wrote powerfully of this privilege of confessing our sins to one another:

> Sin demands to have a man by himself. It withdraws him from the community. The more isolated a person is, the more destructive will be the power of sin over him, and the more deeply he becomes involved in it, the more disastrous is his isolation. Sin wants to remain unknown. It shuns the light. In the darkness of the unexpressed it poisons the whole being of a person. This can happen even in the midst of a pious community. In confession the light of the Gospel breaks into the darkness and seclusion of the heart. The sin must be brought into the light. The unexpressed must be openly spoken and acknowledged. All that is secret and hidden is made manifest. It is a hard struggle until the sin is openly admitted. But God breaks gates of brass and bars of iron.[5]

Confessing our sins to one another results in a purer fellowship of people who know and love one another—who understand one another's needs, anxieties, and temptations. What strength resides in such a community!

Here is a key principle that all Christian communities should operate by: "If a Christian is overcome by some sin, you who are godly should gently and humbly help him back onto the right path, remembering that next time it might be one of you who is in the wrong" (Gal. 6:1 TLB). Pick him or her up and say, "Let me show you from the Word of God what is going on. Let's pray together. Let's walk on the right track together." That is restorative care. We as Christians haven't done our duty if we only rebuke. We need to come alongside and restore—in love.

That verse is perhaps the clearest example from Scripture of how we as believers are to look out for one another. In attacking anxiety, be encouraged to know that angels are looking out for you, but also *make a point* of knowing and being known by mature believers in a context of minstering to each other. The responsibility of finding such a fellowship is yours. Never underestimate the power of godly fellowship in bearing the burden of your anxieties.

# 6

# DEALING WITH
# PROBLEM PEOPLE

ℭ

I n the last chapter, we saw how others can help us in our fight against anxiety. I trust you were impressed by what a precious thing true Christian fellowship is. Here, however, I want to provide a reality check, for Christians don't claim for a moment that the church is perfect. In fact, it's been well said that the church is the only society in the world in which membership is based on the single qualification that the candidate be unworthy of membership.

The church is full of problems because it is full of problem people. Everyone in it is a sinner, albeit saved by grace, but nonetheless influenced by unredeemed human flesh. The church grows spiritually in direct proportion to how well we deal with anxiety and other sins in our midst.

The apostle Paul identified the problem groups we all will encounter in the church. See whether yourself or others come to mind: "We urge you, brethren, admonish the unruly, encourage the fainthearted [the anxious], help the weak, be patient with all men. See that no one repays another with evil for evil, but always seek after that which is good for one another and for all men" (1 Thess. 5:14–15).

Group number one is "the unruly." Let's call them the wayward. They're never in step. "Get with the program" is a slogan that suits them. When everyone else is moving ahead, they're going backward. Out of either apathy or rebellion, they've gone spiritually AWOL, and they're not interested in learning or serving.

Group number two is "the fainthearted"—the worriers. They fear the unknown and have no sense of adventure. Their slogan in the church is "We've never done it that way before." They hate change; they love tradition; they want no risk. All the issues of life seem far more than they can bear. They're usually sad, perpetually worried, sometimes in despair, and often depressed or discouraged. Consequently, they experience none of the thrill that adventure brings.

The third group is "the weak." These believers are spiritually and morally weak. Because of weak self-discipline, they tend to fall into the same sins over and over. You barely get them up on their feet and dust them off when suddenly they're back in the same hole again. They find it hard to do God's will consistently. They embarrass themselves, their church, and their Lord. Thus they require a lot of attention.

The fourth group could be called "the wearisome." Paul said to "be patient with all men." Some people we encounter require an extra degree of patience. You can pour your energy into them, and when you look to see how close they might be to the overall goal of Christlikeness (Phil. 3:12–15), they seem further away. Everything distracts them—they are not focused individuals. They're very exasperating because you make the maximum effort and get the minimum return. They don't grow at a normal pace.

Group five is the outright wicked. Even though Paul was addressing Christians, he found it necessary to say, "See that no one repays another with evil for evil, but always seek after that which is good for one another" (1 Thess. 5:15). There are, sad to say, Christians who commit sins against other Christians. They break up marriages. They defile daughters. They steal. They gossip. They slander. They falsely accuse.

If a church is to grow, it must minister to all five groups. This applies to you: Going to church is not just showing up on Sunday morning. The Lord would have you understand these groups of people so that—much more than not being numbered among their ranks—you might use your spiritual gifts to help them. Then they, in turn, will be able to help others. Help a worrier not to worry, and your own worries disappear in the process. What's more, there's less of a climate of worry in the church. That is an effective way to attack anxiety.

## THE WAYWARD

I learned several key lessons about life when I was in athletics. One is that benchwarmers tend to become critics. The people who do the most criticizing do the least to advance the efforts of the team. I remember having the privilege of being a starting running back. That meant there were others who didn't start because I did. At first they encouraged me, thinking they would get their moment. When they didn't see it coming, they began secretly wishing I would break my leg.

And when I didn't break my leg, they decried the idiocy of the coach, who obviously didn't know talent when he saw it. Eventually, they started rooting for the other team!

That's the progression of the wayward. You see it all the time in the church. Perhaps their way of sitting on the bench is moving farther back in the pews, hanging out on the fringes. They're the first to cut out when the service ends. Either out of apathy or rebellion, they resist involvement. They are unwilling to go beyond an audience mentality.

How are we to deal with such people? Scripture says to admonish the wayward. The Greek term employed (*noutheteō*) means "to put sense into in light of the consequences." If you know believers who are not doing their duty—not using their gifts, not being supportive of the team effort—come alongside those individuals and try to put some sense into their heads. One way to do that is to speak softly and say, "I've been noticing you haven't been faithful in your attendance, you're not involved in a ministry, and you tend to criticize the church. You realize, don't you, that if you continue in that path, there are spiritual consequences, and I don't think you want those consequences, nor do I want you to experience them."

It's to be a gentle, loving warning, yet also have some passion in it. That's how the apostle Paul warned the elders of the Ephesian church: "with tears" (Acts 20:31). There's a hurt in it that says, "I don't want you to keep going in that direction because God *will* punish apathy and rebellion." When you truly love someone, you don't hesitate to warn him or her. I don't hesitate to do that with my wife and children and others who are close to me. It's not because of some agenda I've got, but because I don't want them to have to deal with the inevitable consequences of being spiritually aloof. I want them and everyone else in the church to know the fullness of God's blessing.

This confrontation is necessary. The point of coming to church isn't sitting and staring at the back of someone's head. It's a fellowship; it's being involved in the lives of fellow believers—including the troublesome ones.

## THE FAINTHEARTED

These individuals aren't on the fringes; they're huddled in the middle. They don't want to get near the edge—it's too scary! They need encouragement from God's Word, which is the solution to anxiety.

Paul described these anxious believers as "the fainthearted" (Gk., *oligopsuchos*). That term comes from two words meaning "small" and "soul." The opposite term, *megalopsuchos*, is commonly translated "great souled."

Mohandas Gandhi, who is usually thought of as a humble man, chose to identify himself by the Sanskrit form of *megalopsuchos*, which is *mahatma*. It refers to a person who embraces the massive problems and needs of humanity, who takes great risks because there is great principle and truth at stake. This person is bold, has a sense of adventure, and loves the battle even before tasting the victory.

The *oligopsuchos* is not at all like that. Challenges threaten such individuals. They certainly don't thrive on them. Since they like what is familiar, they tend to cling to traditions. They are reluctant to do anything that hasn't been done before; they love what is safe. They want a risk-free life with absolute security.

Since absolute security is impossible in this life, they're usually depressed. They lack the strength to move out with the church and try new ministries. Because they fear persecution, they find it difficult to share the gospel. Instead of rising above their problems, they sink under everything. They seem to have a great weight upon them. Consequently, they themselves are like weights that the church needs to drag around.

If you look at the church as a parade, they would be the ones carrying the red flags. Everyone else is moving, and they throw up the stop sign because they lack vision and fear failure. I think deep down in their hearts their hero is Indiana Jones, but they'd be reluctant to admit it. They admire courage and a sense of adventure, but rather than learning to cultivate those virtues, they find it much easier to fall into familiar patterns of anxiety.

How are we to deal with such people? Paul said simply to encourage them. The Greek term pictures speaking to someone side by side. If you know someone who's fearful, worried, melancholy, depressed, or despairing, the Lord wants you to come alongside and develop a friendly relationship with him or her. If you tend to be that way yourself, develop friendships with godly people who will console, comfort, strengthen, reassure, cheer, refresh, and soothe you from God's Word. You will be a different person because such relationships bring relief from anxiety.

What kinds of encouragement bring the most relief? The encouragement of prayer to the God of all encouragement, the encouragement of a secure salvation, the encouragement of our sovereign God working out *everything* for the believer's good, the encouragement of the love of Christ, the encouragement of the final resurrection and the righting of all wrongs. All that and more help the worried to participate in the adventure of life.

## The Weak

Paul next said to "help the weak" (1 Thess. 5:14). Being weak in faith is one aspect of this problem. It characterizes believers who are so hypersensitive to sin that they see things as sin that aren't really sin at all. Paul described such people as weaker brothers in his letters to the Roman and Corinthian Christians (Rom. 14–15; 1 Cor. 8). He implored these churches to be sensitive to their concerns.

Often these individuals come to Christ out of a particularly sinful lifestyle. They fear that anything associated with that lifestyle might drag them back into their old habits. They are susceptible to a wounded conscience that could lead them into more sin and more weakness. Therefore, they must not be pushed into doing anything they don't think is right, even though Scripture gives no definitive yes or no about it. With help, largely in the form of patient instruction, they will understand the Word of God more perfectly over time (cf. Acts 18:24–28).

Another group of people who could be classified as weak is those who keep falling into the same sins over and over again. They are morally weak. I think James had them in mind when he said, "Is anyone among you sick? Let him call for the elders of the church, and let them pray over him" (James 5:14). The word translated "sick" is the same one translated "weak" in 1 Thessalonians 5:14. When you're feeling weak spiritually and morally, seek out those who are strong in the faith and ask for their prayer support.

In addition to prayer, the weak need "help" (1 Thess. 5:14). Paul used a Greek term that means "to hold tightly to," "cling to," "support," and "hold up." Here's what it looks like in action: "Brethren, even if a man is caught in any trespass, you who are spiritual, restore such a one in a spirit of gentleness; looking to yourself, lest you too be tempted. Bear one another's burdens, and thus fulfill the law of Christ" (Gal. 6:1–2). We help the weak by picking them up and then holding them up.

How do we do that? Again, intimacy in the fellowship is required. The church grows when the sheep help take care of the sheep—when we care enough to admonish the wayward, encourage the worried, and help the weak. That type of ministry necessitates involvement in people's lives.

## THE WEARISOME

"Be patient with all men," Paul said. It's easy to get frustrated, angry, and exasperated with some people. You can give so much and receive so little in return. That's especially common in discipleship relationships. If you've discipled people over the years, you know what it is like to have a major disappointment.

No one knew that better than Jesus. You can almost hear the exasperation in His voice when He said, "Oh you of little faith!" You'll find that exclamation many times in the Gospels. It's like Jesus was saying to His disciples, "When are you guys gonna get what I've been trying to tell you all this time?" But He was patient with them, and in time they blossomed.

There are many pastors who have survived the wayward, the worried, and the weak, but who have been sacrificed on the altar of the exasperating. They just finally cave in, saying to themselves, *I'm pouring my whole life into these people and the faster I move, the further ahead I get. I can't seem to get them moving with me! They've been trained, but they don't do what we've trained them to do. Neither do they live the way we've taught them to live.*

Whether you're a pastor or not, how would the Lord have you respond to wearisome people? By being patient with them. How patient? More patient than you've been. Think how patient God has been with you. In fact, God describes Himself as "compassionate and gracious, slow to anger" (Ex. 34:6). Patience is a communicable attribute of God, which means it should also characterize His children.

Recall this interchange between Peter and Jesus: "Lord, how often shall my brother sin against me and I forgive him? Up to seven times?" Jesus said to him, "I do not say to you, up to seven times, but up to seventy times seven" (Matt. 18:21–22). Since the religious leaders of the day said to forgive up to three times, Peter must have thought he was being exceptionally generous by suggesting over twice that amount. But Jesus presented some mind-boggling multiplication of His own, all to communicate a spirit of ongoing patience with wearisome Christians who keep doing the same thing to us over and over again. Such compassion and personal love change people—even the wearisome.

## THE WICKED

This group has a whole verse dedicated to it: "See that no one repays another with evil for evil, but always seek after that which is good for one another and for all men" (1 Thess. 5:15). The assumption here is that since God is forbidding vengeance, someone did something evil to you. This, I believe, is the most difficult circumstance we as Christians face—when we suffer painful treatment and abuse not from the world, but from our own brothers and sisters in Christ. It can cause the deepest pain, but our Christian faith must work at this level too.

Be prepared: There are people in the church who will hurt you. They'll harm you directly by attacking you face-to-face with wicked words. They'll harm you indirectly by gossiping and slandering you behind your back. They might eliminate you from their social circle or keep you out of a ministry because of jealousy, bitterness, or anger. They might steal your virtue through sexual sin, break up your marriage, or influence one of your children toward sin. This is malicious harm we're talking about here!

Believers who could even contemplate doing such terrible things to other believers must consider this sober warning:

> Whoever causes one of these little ones who
> believe in Me to stumble, it is better for him that a
> heavy millstone be hung around his neck, and that
> he be drowned in the depth of the sea. Woe to the
> world because of its stumbling-blocks! For it is
> inevitable that stumbling-blocks come; but woe to
> that man through whom the stumbling-block
> comes! … See that you do not despise one of
> these little ones, for I say to you, that their angels
> in heaven continually behold the face of My Father
> who is in heaven. (Matt. 18:6–7, 10)

The context of the passage makes it clear that these "little ones" are believers—children of God—not just children in general. We are so precious to God that the angels keep an eye on His expression as He looks after us. When they see His face wrinkle with concern, they fly off to our aid. They will deal severely with whoever is out to get us. It is a fearsome thing to trifle with God's children.

Nonetheless, some believers will have the audacity to do just that. How are we to respond when we are on the receiving end of their wickedness? Paul said, "See that no one repays another with evil for evil" (1 Thess. 5:15). Don't retaliate.

Only God has the right to retaliate. A text that closely parallels our passage in 1 Thessalonians 5 states this:

> Never pay back evil for evil to anyone. Respect what is right in the sight of all men. If possible, so far as it depends on you, be at peace with all men. Never take your own revenge, beloved, but leave room for the wrath of God, for it is written, "Vengeance is Mine, I will repay, says the Lord." "But if your enemy is hungry, feed him, and if he is thirsty, give him a drink; for in so doing you will heap burning coals upon his head." Do not be overcome by evil, but overcome evil with good. (Rom. 12:17–21)

Perhaps you've thought of a text elsewhere that appears to contradict this teaching. Doesn't the Old Testament grant the right to demand an eye for an eye, a tooth for a tooth, and a life for a life? Yes, but that was a governmental mandate for punishment to fit the crime. It was never a license for personal vengeance. Jesus addressed that misapplication of the governmental mandate, saying essentially, "You've perverted the law of God to the point of thinking you're supposed to hate your enemy. I'm here to tell you God wants you to love your enemy and do good to those who do evil to you" (cf. Matt. 5:43–45).

Obey Jesus by saying to yourself, "These believers ought to know better, but in spite of how wickedly they've treated me, I'm going to return their hostility with goodness." That applies not only to believers, but also to all who mistreat us (with the exception of matters that concern the government). As Paul said it: "Always seek after that which is good for one another and for all men" (1 Thess. 5:15). He expanded on the same concept to the Galatians: "While we have opportunity, let us do good to all men, and especially to those who are of the household of the faith" (Gal. 6:10).

The church does well as a whole when the shepherds and the sheep bond together to correct the wayward, encourage the worried, hold up the weak, be patient with the wearisome, and repay the wicked with love. That is the bigger picture on attacking anxiety.

# HAVING PEACE IN
# EVERY CIRCUMSTANCE

 ﮲

As we saw in the last chapter, Paul closed his first letter to the Thessalonians with practical instructions on ministering to problem people in the church, including the worried. In this chapter we will see how he closed his second letter to them—with a prayer any anxious Christian would love someone to have prayed on his or her behalf: "May the Lord of peace Himself continually grant you peace in every circumstance.... The grace of our Lord Jesus Christ be with you" (3:16, 18).

## A PRAYER FOR GOD'S PEACE

Peace is commonly defined as the sense of calm, tranquility, quietness, bliss, contentment, and well-being that we feel when everything is going the way we'd like it to go. That definition, however, is incomplete because that feeling can also be produced by a pill—or by alcohol, a nap, a generous inheritance, or even deliberate deception. The reassurance of a friend or someone you love whispering sweet nothings into your ear can also produce that kind of peace.

That's not the kind of peace Paul had in mind. Godly peace has nothing to do with human beings or human circumstances. In fact, godly peace cannot be produced on a human level at all. Any peace that can be produced by humans is very fragile. It can be destroyed instantly by failure, doubt, fear, difficulty, guilt, shame, distress, regret, sorrow, the anxiety of making a wrong choice, the anticipation of being mistreated or victimized by someone, the uncertainty of the future, and any challenge to our position or possessions. And we experience these things daily.

The peace that God gives is not subject to the vicissitudes of life. It is a spiritual peace; it is an attitude of heart and mind when we believe and thus know deep down that all is well between ourselves and God. Along with it is the assurance that He is lovingly in control of everything. We as Christians should know for sure that our sins are forgiven, that God is concerned with our well-being, and that heaven is our destiny. God's peace is our possession and privilege by divine right. Let's first consider its origin.

## IT IS DIVINE

This peace is defined for us in several ways in 2 Thessalonians 3:16. To begin with, it is divine: "May the Lord of peace *Himself* ... grant you peace." The Lord of peace is the one who gives it. The pronoun *himself* is emphatic in the Greek text and underscores God's personal involvement. Christian peace, the peace unique to Christians, comes personally from Him. It is the very essence of His nature.

To put it simply, peace is an attribute of God. If I asked you to list the attributes of God, these are the ones that would probably come most readily to mind: His love, grace, mercy, justice, holiness, wisdom, truth, omnipotence, immutability, and immortality. But do you ever think of God as being characterized by peace? In fact, He is peace. Whatever it is that He gives us, He has and He is. There is no lack of perfect peace in His being. God is never stressed. He is never anxious. He never worries. He never doubts. He never fears. God is never at cross-purposes with Himself. He never has problems making up His mind.

God lives in perfect calm and contentment. Why? Because He's in charge of everything and can operate everything perfectly according to His own will. Since He is omniscient, He is never surprised. There are no threats to His omnipotence. There is no possible sin that can stain His holiness. Even His wrath is clear, controlled, and confident. There is no regret in His mind; for He has never done, said, or thought anything that He would change in any way.[1]

God enjoys perfect harmony within Himself. Our Bibles call Him "the Lord of peace," but in the Greek text a definite article appears before the word translated "peace," meaning He literally is "the Lord of *the peace.*" This is real peace—the divine kind—not the kind the world has. Paul's prayer is that we might experience that kind of peace. Its source is God and God alone.

## IT IS A GIFT

Not only is this peace divine in origin, but it is also a gift. When Paul prayed, "Now may the Lord of peace Himself continually grant you peace," the word translated "grant" is the verb meaning "to give." It speaks of a gift. God's peace is a sovereign, gracious gift given to those who believe in the Lord Jesus Christ.

According to Psalm 85:8, a verse you may have never noticed before, the psalmist states, "I will hear what God the LORD will say; for He will speak peace to His people, to His godly ones." God grants peace to those who belong to Him. Jesus said, "My peace I give to you; not as the world gives, do I give to you. Let not your heart be troubled, nor let it be fearful" (John 14:27). There's no greater gift for the anxious than God's peace.

Some, however, will seek relief for their anxieties through a false peace. God is generous to whom He grants His peace, but there is a limit. Isaiah wrote, "'Peace, peace to him who is far and to him who is near,' says the LORD, 'and I will heal him.' But the wicked are like the tossing sea, for it cannot be quiet, and its waters toss up refuse and mud. 'There is no peace,' says my God, 'for the wicked'" (57:19–21). He will grant peace to those who come to Him from near and far—those who grew up hearing much about Him and those who heard little to nothing—but those who don't come to Him, the wicked, enjoy no real peace.

Thomas Watson explains further:

> Peace flows from sanctification, but they being
> unregenerate, have nothing to do with peace....
> They may have a truce, but no peace. God may
> forebear the wicked a while, and stop the roaring
> of his cannon; but though there be a truce, yet
> there is no peace. The wicked may have something

which looks like peace, but it is not. They may be
fearless and stupid; but there is a great difference
between a stupefied conscience, and a pacified
conscience.... This is the devil's peace; he rocks
men in the cradle of security; he cries, Peace,
peace, when men are on the precipice of hell.
The seeming peace a sinner has, is not from the
knowledge of his happiness, but the ignorance of
his danger.[2]

The peace of the wicked is born of delusion. True peace
is the child of saving grace. In a prayer similar to the one that
closes 2 Thessalonians, Paul said, "May the God of hope fill
you with all joy and peace in believing" (Rom. 15:13). Peace
is a gift to those who believe.

### IT IS ALWAYS AVAILABLE

God's peace is the gift that keeps on giving. Another way to
express that truth is how Paul said it: "May the Lord of
peace ... continually grant you peace" (2 Thess. 3:16). By
adding "continually," Paul was emphasizing that it is con-
stantly available. The implication is, however, that it can be
interrupted.

It isn't God who interrupts our spiritual peace, but us. We
can suspend the flow of peace in our lives by giving in to our
flesh, which is still part of this world. Unless we "walk by the
Spirit," our means of controlling the flesh (Gal. 5:16), we are
open season to all kinds of anxieties: the dread of the
unknown, the fear of disease and death—and we all can list a
string of others. How does this unfortunate process begin?
When we stop focusing on our permanent condition in Christ,

who will certainly bring us into His glory, and when we start basing our happiness on the fleeting things of the world, those things by definition will change. Thus, if we get upset when they do, we will spend our lives in distress.

People who can ride through the toughest issues of life and remain calm are not indifferent; they're just trusting God. What if our ride is a little bumpy? What if we're feeling troubled, anxious, and fearful? How can we restore the peace? How can it remain uninterrupted?

The psalmist said to himself, "Why are you in despair, O my soul? And why have you become disturbed within me? Hope in God, for I shall yet praise Him, the help of my countenance, and my God" (Ps. 42:11). He reminded himself that God was there to help him. We can trust Him because He is trustworthy. He genuinely cares for us.

Long ago, God made it perfectly clear to Israel that peace comes from obeying His Word (Lev. 26:1–6). The same truth applies today. Peace is restored through obedience. The first step is to turn away from sin. Sometimes the sin is the doubt, fear, or anxiety itself, but also it can be an underlying sin that has produced those feelings. Probe your heart and isolate the cause of its unrest. Give up the sin that has been revealed to you and obey God by applying the opposite virtue. In the case of anxiety, that means having faith in God to help you manage life's details.

Something else that will restore your peace is to accept whatever stresses or challenges God has seen fit to bring into your life. In the book of Job we read:

> Behold, how happy is the man whom God
> reproves, so do not despise the discipline of the
> Almighty. For He inflicts pain, and gives relief;

He wounds, and His hands also heal.... In
famine He will redeem you from death, and in
war from the power of the sword. You will be
hidden from the scourge of the tongue, neither
will you be afraid of violence when it comes.
You will laugh at violence and famine, neither
will you be afraid of wild beasts. For you will be
in league with the stones of the field; and the
beasts of the field will be at peace with you.
And you will know that your tent is secure, for
you will visit your abode and fear no loss.
(5:17–18, 20–24)

If you understand that God is using all the difficulties you
face to perfect you, you'll be at peace. It is not all for nothing. You may not always know why you're going through
this or that, but be encouraged that there is a good reason.
Turning to the New Testament, you'll see Paul said if you
want peace, do good (Rom. 2:10). All who do good will
enjoy peace. To be more specific, "the wisdom from above is
first pure, then peaceable.... And the seed whose fruit is
righteousness is sown in peace by those who make peace"
(James 3:17–18). Living according to the Word—according
to heavenly wisdom, to God's revealed standard of righteousness—brings peace.

If you've lost God's peace in your life, you can find it
again. Retrace your steps by trusting God in everything,
turning away from sin and walking in obedience, enduring His refining work in your life, doing what is good, and
living by the Word of God in a righteous way. As Paul
said, God's peace is continually available to you. Avail
yourself of it.

## *IT IS NOT SUBJECT TO CIRCUMSTANCES*

A final characteristic of God's peace is that it is not subject to circumstances. Paul's prayer was that we might continually enjoy it "in every circumstance" (2 Thess. 3:16). This peace is not subject to anything that happens in the worldly realm. It is not built on any human relationship. It is not built on any human circumstance. Rather, it is built on an unchanging divine relationship and a divine plan and promise from an unfailing God who will secure you in Himself and who will do everything for your good. This peace is unbreakable, unassailable, transcendent.

As we noted earlier, Jesus said, "Peace I leave with you; My peace I give to you; not as the world gives, do I give to you. Let not your heart be troubled, nor let it be fearful" (John 14:27). He was saying, "There's nothing to fear or be anxious about because I'm giving you a transcendent peace that—unlike the world's peace—is unassailable by any human circumstance." We demonstrate that Jesus keeps His promises when, in the midst of worldly upheavals that would normally tear us up and trouble our lives, we remain calm.

## A PRAYER FOR GOD'S GRACE

Paul's great desire was that we enjoy that kind of well-being, which is why he prayed toward that end. His parting wish was this: "The grace of our Lord Jesus Christ be with you all" (2 Thess. 3:18). He wanted every man and woman who would ever put his or her faith in Christ to experience the abiding presence of God's grace.

Grace is God's goodness or benevolence given to those who don't deserve it. "Grace and truth were realized through

Jesus Christ" (John 1:17). It was in the person of God's Son that "the grace of God has appeared," making salvation available to all (Titus 2:11). Once we embrace this saving grace through faith in Christ, we are blessed with God's grace enabling us to withstand any difficulty that would tend to make us anxious. Paul described this grace while confessing to a difficulty that brought him great anxiety:

> There was given me a thorn in the flesh, a messenger of Satan to buffet me.... Concerning this I entreated the Lord three times that it might depart from me. And He has said to me, "My grace is sufficient for you, for power is perfected in weakness." Most gladly, therefore, I will rather boast about my weaknesses, that the power of Christ may dwell in me. Therefore I am well content with weaknesses, with insults, with distresses, with persecutions, with difficulties, for Christ's sake; for when I am weak, then I am strong. (2 Cor. 12:7–10)

As believers, we also are blessed with the grace that equips us for divine service. Paul expressed his appreciation for this grace in saying, "I thank Christ Jesus our Lord, who has strengthened me, because He considered me faithful, putting me into service; even though I was formerly a blasphemer and a persecutor and a violent aggressor. And yet I was shown mercy.... The grace of our Lord was more than abundant" (1 Tim. 1:12–14).

Grace is what enables us to grow spiritually in the knowledge of our Lord and Savior Jesus Christ (2 Peter 3:18). In the material realm, Paul appealed to God's grace in encouraging the Corinthian church to be generous in giving to the Lord's work: "God is able to make all grace abound to you, that always having all sufficiency in everything, you may have an abundance for every good deed" (2 Cor. 9:8).

God's grace saves us, helps us cope with our anxieties, equips us for service, and enables us to grow spiritually and to be rich in God. Like God's peace, it is always available, and there is no limit to it. And again, like God's peace, the conditions for receiving it are trusting God, turning from sin, enduring the refining process, doing good, and living by the Word. As we are what we ought to be, God infuses us with His peace and grace. And that has a wonderful way of crowding out anxiety.

I want to end this chapter on a personal note. A few days after presenting *this very message* to my congregation at Grace Church, I had an unprecedented opportunity to apply it to my own life: I was notified that my wife and youngest daughter were in a serious auto accident and that my wife, Patricia, would probably die. Everything seemed like a blur to me, the details frustratingly sketchy—I was afraid she was already dead. During my hour-long drive to the hospital, I had a lot of time to reflect on the severity of the situation. Yet I experienced a deep and settled peace simply because I knew God had not failed me—His grace was at work in my family's lives, and He was in complete control. I am happy to report that God spared both their lives and that Patricia has recovered beautifully. If you too rely on God's grace, He will see you through the most difficult trials.

# DOING ALL THINGS
# WITHOUT COMPLAINING

ᏨᎭ

One of the first biblical passages we examined on anxiety was Paul's straightforward command in Philippians 4:6: "Be anxious for nothing." In the last two chapters of this book, we will probe two other passages from Philippians. One comes before the command, and the other comes afterward. They bracket our understanding of how to attack anxiety by specifying a habit to avoid and an attitude to cultivate. Follow through with what you learn and you will see for yourself that Paul wasn't issuing an impossible command.

Our first text is: "Do all things without grumbling or disputing; that you may prove yourselves to be blameless and innocent, children of God above reproach in the midst of a crooked and perverse generation, among whom you

appear as lights in the world, holding fast the word of life"
(Phil. 2:14–16).

## DISCONTENT IN SOCIETY

We live in a society that loves to complain. Ironically, the most
indulged society the world has known thus far is also the most
discontent. The more people have, the more discontent they
are apt to be with what they have—and these types don't
believe in suffering in silence. We seem to be breeding a generation of complainers.

While listening to the radio, I happened to catch a
thought-provoking speech by a sociologist. He was talking
about young people characterized by a complaining attitude,
a distaste for responsibility, and a sullen discontent that nothing is ever the way they would like it. The sociologist put
forth the thesis that this discontented generation is mainly the
product of small families.

Most families in America have either none, one, or two
children. The theory is that small families in a materialistic
society are apt to breed selfish, self-indulgent children.
Picture this scene at the breakfast table: The mother asks
her one or two children, "What would you like me to fix
you to take to school for lunch?" One says peanut butter,
the other says tuna. She says OK and starts preparing cus-
tomized lunches. When the kids are about to go off to
school, she asks, "What would you like for dinner when you
come home?" The first kid: "Oh well, I guess I'd like this
..." The second kid: " ... and I'd like that." "OK," Mom
responds, "I'll have this for you and that for you. By the
way, what time will you be home? What time should I plan
dinner?" The kids collaborate and say, "Let's see, we'll

probably be home somewhere between four and five. Better make it five thirty."

If you are raised in a family with three children or more, a different reality is apt to prevail. When you get up in the morning and make it down to the kitchen, you get handed a bag. And when you leave the house, your mother says to you, "Dinner is at five thirty. You're here, you eat."

At the dinner table in a small family, the mother may have practically broken her back to prepare some exotic cuisine. After taking one bite, at least one of the kids will probably say, "I don't like it. I want something else." If one child in a family of five or six children makes that comment, the kid next to him or her says, "Good!" and gobbles it up.

The difference is that in most small families in America, authority defers to the child. In most large families—mainly because of logistics—the child must defer to authority. So what you have, said the sociologist, is a generation growing up in an environment where authority defers to them. It is the unfortunate product of child-centered parenting.

When I was a child, I looked forward to growing up because I wanted my freedom. I was expected to conform to my surroundings, and I did. I ate what my parents gave me and wore whatever my mother brought home. I don't remember ever going shopping with my mother—I don't think I even entered a department store as a young person! I conformed to the system, which may sound negative at first, but it really wasn't considering the positive effect it produced: I was eager to assume the responsibilities of adulthood so I could be free to make my own choices.

The reverse is now true. Children who grow up controlling the family environment don't want to become adults because that means conformity for them. They don't want to get a job because nobody at work is going to say, "How would you like your office decorated? And what time would you like to break for lunch?" Rather, they put you on an assembly line or in some other place, and you are expected to conform to their rules. No wonder we have a generation of young people who don't want to grow up and leave home!

Ask the average high school or college student what he or she wants to do after graduation, and you'll receive the usual response: "I don't know." The sociologist theorizes that so many of them feel this way because they're postponing responsibility. The freedom of their childhood seems so much more attractive than conformity to a system. Their parents, although usually well meaning, are unwittingly training them to be irresponsible.

When reality hits, when children raised this way are finally forced to get a job, count on them looking for whatever offers the most amount of money for the least amount of work. They have no work ethic or sense of excellence for excellence's sake.[1] The objective of these adult children is to finance themselves so they can indulge in the things they enjoy. An appropriate bumper sticker on their car might read, "He who dies with the most toys wins." They try making the most out of the necessary evil of adulthood by collecting gadgets, boats, cars, vacation trips, and whatever else might reignite the flame of their lost childhood.

That is a hollow pursuit, however, because "not even when one has an abundance does his life consist of his possessions," said Jesus (Luke 12:15). These adult children will feel empty inside and know that something is missing. Rather than seeing it's because they're emphasizing the physical at the expense of the spiritual, most will assume it's because they don't have enough—and whatever they have is never enough to these individuals! Moreover, their attitude is infectious, and that's why our society tends to be critical.

The complaints have become more and more petty over time. Think about the things most people complain about, get anxious over, and even become enraged over. You may feel convicted. I know I've been guilty of letting some of these things bother me more than they should. Something as commonplace as a traffic jam can bring on incredible anger. Slow drivers in front of us and people who cut us off can be enough to make us fall back into sin! Talkative people irritate us. Long lines, short lines—any lines—drive us crazy. We want it our way, and we want it now!

Think how distressed people become over crying babies. Rather than accepting them as part of life, a terrible brooding discontent has led to a frightening increase in child abuse. Phone calls at inconvenient times, misplaced keys, nonhousebroken puppies, stuck zippers, tight clothes, unsuccessful diets, being rushed or interrupted by someone—we get distressed by the biggies, don't we?

Now if we're in Hiroshima and it's 1945, we have a problem worthy of considerable concern. But just because we lost out on a promotion, a business deal, or something else we wanted doesn't mean we're to complain about it and become anxious. We can surely find a way to survive, calm down, and review the situation. Our concerns are productive when they lead to a sensible course of action, but not when they lead to anxiety. Be aware that our concerns are far more apt to follow the path to anxiety and misery if accompanied by complaints.

It is a sin to complain against God, and we must see our complaints as such. "Who are you, O man, who answers back to God?" asked Paul rhetorically. "The thing molded will not say to the molder, 'Why did you make me like this,' will it?" (Rom. 9:20). Complaining against God is out of place and completely inappropriate. Don't be fooled into thinking only the worst blasphemers commit that sin. Isn't it God we are really complaining against when we gripe about our circumstances? After all, He is the one who put us where we are. A lack of thankfulness and contentment is ultimately an attack on God.

Complainers have a devastating effect on the church. Some are apostates, whom Jude described as "grumblers, finding fault, following after their own lusts" (Jude v. 16). Their sin is so defiling because it is highly contagious. We find abundant proof of that in the Old Testament. Let's consider it carefully so we can protect ourselves and our churches from descending into a morass of complaints, discontentment, anxiety, and misery.

## DISCONTENT IN THE OLD TESTAMENT

This is the scene: The Israelites are in the wilderness, heading toward the Promised Land after God miraculously delivered them from centuries of bondage in Egypt. God tells them to occupy the land. Joshua, Caleb, and ten others spy out the land and give their report:

> Caleb quieted the people before Moses, and said, "We should by all means go up and take possession of it, for we shall surely overcome it." But the men who had gone up with him said, "We are not able to go up against the people, for they are too strong for us." So they gave out to the sons of Israel a bad report of the land which they had spied out, saying,

"The land through which we have gone, in
spying it out, is a land that devours its inhabi-
tants; and all the people whom we saw in it are
men of great size.... We became like grasshop-
pers in our own sight, and so we were in their
sight."

Then all the congregation ... grumbled
against Moses and Aaron; and ... said to them,
"Would that we had died in the land of Egypt!
Or would that we had died in this wilderness!
And why is the Lord bringing us into this land,
to fall by the sword? Our wives and our little
ones will become plunder; would it not be better for us to return to Egypt?" So they said to
one another, "Let us appoint a leader and
return to Egypt."

Then Moses and Aaron fell on their faces in
the presence of all the assembly.... And Joshua
... and Caleb ... spoke to all the congregation
of the sons of Israel, saying, "... Do not rebel
against the Lord; and do not fear the people of
the land.... Their protection has been removed
from them, and the Lord is with us...." But all
the congregation said to stone them with
stones. (Num. 13:30—14:7, 9–10)

Those ten spies, those prophets of doom, kicked off
nationwide discontent by complaining against what God
had commanded them to do. What does Scripture say happened to them? "As for the men whom Moses sent to spy
out the land and who returned and made all the congregation grumble ... even those men who brought out the very

bad report of the land died by a plague before the LORD" (Num. 14:36–37). Does that give you an idea of what God thinks about grumblers? They spread a noxious poison that quickly infects other people. They have the capability of setting into motion a group panic attack.

That happened many times in Israel's history. Poor Moses had to suffer complaints regularly about his leadership and the food God provided for the people. According to Psalm 106, the complaints of the Israelites "tempted God in the desert.... They despised the pleasant land; they did not believe in His word, but grumbled in their tents.... Therefore He swore to them, that He would cast them down in the wilderness, and that He would cast their seed among the nations" (vv. 14, 24–27). That divine judgment has dogged their nation throughout its history.

The New Testament makes it clear that the church is to learn from Israel's mistake. After describing the incredible blessings Israel enjoyed from God's hand, Paul stated, "Nevertheless, with most of them God was not well pleased; for they were laid low in the wilderness. Now these things [are] examples for us, that we should not crave evil things, as they also craved ... nor grumble, as some of them did, and were destroyed" (1 Cor. 10:5–6, 10).

Complaining is the symptom of a deep-seated spiritual problem—a failure to trust God and submit to His will. It is not a trivial matter: "The one who does not believe God has made Him a liar" (1 John 5:10). Here's a better text to adhere to: "Why should any living mortal ... offer complaint in view of his sins?" (Lam. 3:39). God has forgiven our sins, and the only proper way to say thank you is to be grateful. As we learned previously, a spirit of thanksgiving drives away anxiety—and also makes it hard to complain.

*Disputing = questioning & criticizing*

## CONTENTMENT AS A COMMAND

We now have the background for understanding Paul's command in Philippians 2:14: "Do all things without grumbling or disputing." The "all things" refers back to what Paul had said previously: "Work out your salvation with fear and trembling; for it is God who is at work in you" (vv. 12–13). In other words, while God is working in your life, be sure you never complain.

Life isn't always going to serve us what we'd like. God will allow trials in our lives to help us pray, trust, and be grateful for what we have. Through it all the Bible commands us to be content:

- Luke 3:14: "Be content with your wages."
- 1 Timothy 6:6, 8: "Godliness with contentment is great gain.... If we have food and clothing, we will be content with that" (NIV).
- Hebrews 13:5: "Let your way of life be free from the love of money, being content with what you have."

*Roadblocks to Contentment = grumbling & disputing*

Two roadblocks to contentment are grumbling and disputing. The Greek word translated "grumbling" in Philippians 2:14 is *gongusmos*. It's a grouchy, grumbly, onomatopoeic word. It sounds as grumpy as its meaning. It refers to murmuring, an expression of discontent and muttering in a low voice. It's the word used in the Greek translation of the Old Testament to describe the grumblings of Israel. It's a complaint expressed with a negative attitude, an emotional rejection of God's will.

The Greek word translated "disputing" (*dialogismos*) is more intellectual in nature. It refers to questioning and criticism.

*A better way to live = live out your Christian life without questioning criticizing & complaining.*

This is when emotional bellyaching turns into a debate with God (as it did with Job). We start arguing with God about why things are the way they are or why we have to do what we're supposed to do. We think we have a better idea than God about the job, marriage, church, home, or any other situation we're in.

Paul said there's a better way to live—working out our Christian life without complaining. It's an attitude more in tune with life as it is. We are living in a fallen world. It isn't always going to be the way we like it, and the people around us aren't always going to be the way we'd like them to be. When we complain about them, we offend God and position ourselves for His judgment. James warned, "Do not complain, brethren, against one another, that you yourselves may not be judged; behold, the Judge is standing right at the door" (James 5:9). Imagine a little kid in his room complaining to his sister, "Boy, I sure hate the way Dad treats us." But what he doesn't know is that Dad is standing right outside the door! God, likewise, is always in earshot of our complaints.

## THE REASONS BEHIND THE COMMAND

It would be wrong to conclude, however, that God is always waiting to get us. In His Word He not only tells us that He hates complaining, but He also makes it very clear why. He wants us to see that the reasons are as dear to our own hearts as to His and are clearly in our best interests.

### STOP COMPLAINING FOR YOUR OWN SAKE

Paul said not to complain so we "may prove [ourselves] to be blameless and innocent, children of God above reproach"

(Phil. 2:15). When we stop complaining, we free ourselves to be all God wants us to be. "Be imitators of God," Paul said, "as beloved children" (Eph. 5:1). If you are a child of God, live the way a child of God should live by manifesting the character of God. A godly life is how we "adorn the doctrine of God our Savior in every respect" (Titus 2:10).

A literal translation of the Greek text in Philippians 2:14–15 is: "Stop complaining in order that you may become blameless, innocent children of God." There is a process here. Salvation has past, present, and future aspects to it. These verses refer to the present aspect. As God does His work in us, our part is not to complain.

The words translated "blameless," "innocent," and "above reproach" all speak of moral purity. A blameless person is one who cannot be justly criticized. An innocent person is "wise in what is good, and innocent in what is evil" (Rom. 16:19)—and very careful with what he or she allows himself or herself to be exposed to. A person who is "above reproach" is literally spotless, a reference to a sacrifice that is acceptable to God. These verses are saying we're to act in the way God's children are expected to act.

Ask yourself a couple of questions: *Whom do I belong to? Whose name do I bear?* As Christians, we are to live consistently with who we are. I remember as a boy getting caught in a compromising situation and having a deacon at my father's church say to me, "Don't you know who your father is? [He was the pastor.] How can you act like that?" That has stuck in my mind as a spiritual truth. It helps me resolve not to conduct myself in any way that might cause someone to say, "Don't you know who your heavenly Father is? How can you act like that?" Keep that in mind the next time you're tempted to become anxious or complain. Hold your

head up high and realize that God has destined you for
something better. You have been created to reflect His
nature.

## STOP COMPLAINING FOR THE SAKE OF NON-CHRISTIANS

Paul explained that we reflect God's nature to "prove [our-
selves] to be ... children of God above reproach in the midst
of a crooked and perverse generation, among whom [we]
appear as lights in the world, holding fast the word of life"
(Phil. 2:15–16). How we live has a dramatic effect not only
on whether we're consistent with who we are as children of
God, but also on how we affect the world around us.

This statement addresses our evangelistic mandate and is
the heart of Paul's appeal. A simple definition of evangelism
is God's children shining as lights in a dark world. Doing that
effectively involves two things: content and character. It's not
just what we say but what we are.

"In the midst of a crooked and perverse generation" is a
phrase borrowed from the Song of Moses in Deuteronomy
32:5. Moses used it to describe the generation of complainers
who perished in the wilderness. Here it is applied to the society of the world in which the church exists now. Like Israel of
old, it rejects God's message. It therefore is a tragic world,
morally warped and spiritually perverted.

The Greek word translated "crooked" is *skolios*. Perhaps
you've heard of scoliosis of the spine. It's an improper cur-
vature of the spine, appropriately named since the Greek
term describes anything that is out of proper alignment and
that deviates from the standard. According to Proverbs
2:15, the lost are those "whose paths are crooked, and who
are devious in their ways." The prophet Isaiah put it this

*a murmuring, complaining, discontented grumbling griping Christian will never have a positive influence on others.*

way: "All we like sheep have gone astray" (53:6 KJV). Humanity has a spiritual disease, a scoliosis of the heart that moves people away from the straight plumb line of God's revealed righteousness.

The word translated "perverse" amplifies how far off the standard they really are. It refers to something that has been severely twisted and distorted. Think how twisted our society has become in presenting vices such as homosexuality and abortion not only as right, but also as fundamental rights to be protected. As believers we are to shine as lights to such a world.

If you are a godly, obedient Christian, you will have an almost startling effect on most people. They will feel the light, and some may even shy away from it because it is so obvious that you possess something they don't possess. Others will be attracted to it because they have a yearning to be something better than what they are. Their fate is inextricably intertwined with how we live our lives. As John Donne wrote hauntingly, "No man is an island, entire of itself" ("Meditation 17"). That is especially true of the Christian. A few sentences later Donne affirmed, "I am involved in mankind." For the Christian, that is more than a resolve; it is a statement of fact.

The quality of your life is the platform of your personal testimony. A murmuring, discontent, grumbling, griping, and complaining Christian is never going to have a positive influence on others. It's incongruous to be talking about the gospel of forgiveness, joy, peace, and comfort, yet be moaning and complaining much of the time. Give people more credit than that: They aren't going to believe the gospel until they see it do what you say it will do. "Show me your redeemed lives, and I might be inclined to believe in your Redeemer" is a valid challenge for any non-Christian to make.

As I said earlier, the equation for evangelism is character plus content. While appearing as lights in the world, we simultaneously are to be "holding fast the word of life" (Phil. 2:16). It is the Word of God that gives life. Since the people of the world are spiritually dead in their sins (Eph. 2:1), there is nothing they need more.

Stop grumbling, said Paul. Stop arguing with God. Obey Him joyfully. In the process of shining as lights in the world, you will find there will be a ready reception, because a transformed life is the greatest advertisement for the gospel. A negative, griping, complaining spirit is the worst.

Try your best to make it through today without complaining about something. Make a note *every* time you do complain. You may be surprised to discover it has become a way of life. In addition to being highly contagious to others, a complaining spirit has an anesthetic effect on whoever possesses it. It quickly becomes so habitual that most people infected by it don't even realize what a dominant characteristic it has become.

Put a check on the complaints you utter, and you will succeed in attacking anxiety at its source. You will be affirming that God knows what He is doing in your life. To hear yourself complain is to hear yourself affirm the contrary. The more you hear yourself talk like that, the more you'll believe it. For peace of mind, stop it now.

*Stop complaining and you will succeed in attacking anxiety at its source.*

# LEARNING TO BE CONTENT

As white is to black, so is contentment to complaints and anxiety. All along we have been developing an arsenal to draw on in attacking anxiety, and now we close by focusing on our most essential weapon. The Christian's Excalibur against the dragon Anxiety is named Contentment. It likewise is the banner under which Christ's troops advance to personal victory.

As we saw earlier, the Bible speaks of contentment not only as a virtue but also as a command. Nowhere is that clearer than in Paul's closing comments to the Philippian church. He had just told them never to succumb to anxiety (Phil. 4:6) and then went on to illustrate how with a glimpse from his own life:

> I rejoiced in the Lord greatly, that ... you have
> revived your concern for me; indeed, you were

concerned before, but you lacked opportunity. Not that I speak from want; for I have learned to be content in whatever circumstances I am. I know how to get along with humble means, and I also know how to live in prosperity; in any and every circumstance I have learned the secret of being filled and going hungry, both of having abundance and suffering need. I can do all things through Him who strengthens me. Nevertheless, you have done well to share with me in my afflic-tion. And you yourselves also know, Philippians, that at the first preaching of the gospel, after I departed from Macedonia, no church shared with me in the matter of giving and receiving but you alone; for even in Thessalonica you sent a gift more than once for my needs. Not that I seek the gift itself, but I seek for the profit which increases to your account. But I have received everything in full, and have an abundance; I am amply sup-plied, having received from Epaphroditus what you have sent, a fragrant aroma, an acceptable sacrifice, well pleasing to God. And my God shall supply all your needs according to His riches in glory in Christ Jesus. (vv. 10–19)

In the context of this inspired thank-you note, it is clear Paul knew what it was to be content. At the time of this writ-ing Paul was a prisoner under house arrest in Rome. He was chained to a Roman soldier twenty-four hours a day. He had little of what this life considers benefits, but still he was con-tent. "The peace of God" (v. 7) and "the God of peace" (v. 9) were obvious realities in Paul's life. They can likewise be in ours as we learn how to be content.

## INDEPENDENCE, NOT INDIFFERENCE

The Greek word translated "content" (*autarkēs*) means "to be self-sufficient," "to be satisfied," "to have enough." It indicates a certain independence and lack of need for help. Sometimes it was used to refer to a person who supported himself or herself without anyone's aid.

Paul was saying, "I have learned to be sufficient in myself—yet not in myself as myself, but as indwelt by Christ." He elsewhere expressed that subtle distinction: "I have been crucified with Christ; and it is no longer I who live, but Christ lives in me; and the life which I now live in the flesh I live by faith in the Son of God, who loved me, and delivered Himself up for me" (Gal. 2:20). Christ and contentment go together.

The Stoic philosophers of Paul's day had a different view of contentment. Stoicism was a Greek philosophy introduced in Rome around 200 BC. There it attracted such notable followers as Epictetus and Seneca, tutor of Emperor Nero. It was Nero who later ordered Paul's execution. The Stoics held that all reality is material, and they stressed putting aside passion and extravagance to perform one's duty and gain true freedom. (Self-indulgent Nero made a lousy Stoic!) They believed *autarkēs*, or contentment, was achieved only when one came to the point of total indifference. Epictetus explains how to go about reaching this exalted state:

> Begin with a cup or a household utensil. If it breaks, say, "I don't care." Go on to a horse or pet dog. If anything happens to it, say, "I don't

care." Go on to yourself and if you're hurt or
injured in any way, say, "I don't care." And if
you go on long enough and if you try hard
enough, you'll come to a state when you can
watch your nearest and dearest suffer and die
and say, "I don't care."[1]

The Stoics attempted to abolish their feelings and emotions. Frankly, that sounds more like something out of *Star
Trek* and Vulcan philosophy than anything that could have
originated from Planet Earth! T. R. Glover said, "The Stoics
made of the heart a desert and called it peace."[2]

That's not the kind of contentment Paul was talking
about. When he used the word *autarkēs* he was referring to
something very different. It obviously wasn't indifference,
for Paul was an intensely compassionate man. His love letters
to the churches throughout the New Testament make that
clear. Paul could *never* assume an "I don't care" attitude!
Under the inspiration of the Holy Spirit he took the idea of
contentment much further than it was taken even in the
Greek culture, where the word first found its meaning. Let's
see where he took it.

## SECRETS TO CONTENTMENT

Notice that Paul said, "I have learned to be content.... I have
learned the secret" (Phil. 4:11–12). Here he used another
Greek term pregnant with meaning—an allusion to the mys-
tery religions of Greece. Initiation into those pagan cults
involved becoming privy to certain religious secrets. Paul
became privy to the secret of contentment, and it's one he

passed on to all who have been initiated by faith in Jesus Christ. Here are its key facets:

## CONFIDENCE IN GOD'S PROVIDENCE

Paul said, "I rejoiced in the Lord greatly, that ... you have revived your concern for me; indeed, you were concerned before, but you lacked opportunity" (v. 10). Let me give you some background. About ten years had passed since Paul was last in Philippi. Acts 16 relates what happened during his first visit.

Paul and his traveling companions met a businesswoman named Lydia and preached the gospel to her and her companions. Their conversion resulted in the formation of a church. During the early days of that church, Paul cast out a spirit of divination from a slave girl. The girl's owners—livid over the loss of the income they had derived from her fortune-telling abilities—had Paul flogged, thrown into prison, and locked in stocks. Instead of complaining about the miserable situation in which he found himself, he praised God through thankful prayer and song far into the night.

God responded in an amazing way: He shook the foundations of the prison so violently that all its doors opened wide and the chains fell off the prisoners' feet and wrists. That incredible experience, plus Paul's incredible response to his dismal circumstances, led to the salvation of the jailer—and the jailer's entire household. As the church at Philippi grew, it's apparent that they helped fund Paul for further missionary outreach.

Our text in Philippians makes it clear, however, that it had been awhile since they last were able to help support him

God is sovereign ordering everything for His own Holy purposes and the ultimate good of those who love Him.

in that endeavor. But that was fine with Paul. He knew it wasn't that they lacked concern, but that they lacked "opportunity" (Gk., *kairos*). That's a reference to a season or window of opportunity, not to chronological time.

In writing, "You have revived your concern for me," Paul was using a horticultural term that means "to bloom again." That's like saying, "Your love has flowered again. I know it has always been there, but it just didn't have an opportunity to bloom. Blooms are seasonal, and the right season hadn't come along until now."

The point is that Paul had a patient confidence in God's sovereign providence. He was content to do without and wait on the Lord's timing. He didn't resort to panic or manipulation of others. Those things are never called for. Paul was certain that in due time God would order the circumstances so that his needs would be met. We can have that same certainty today.

Until we truly learn that God is sovereign, ordering everything for His own holy purposes and the ultimate good of those who love Him, we can't help but be discontent. That's because in taking on the responsibility of ordering our lives, we will be frustrated in repeatedly discovering that we can't control everything. Everything already *is* under control however, by Someone far greater than you or I.

A synonym for God's providence is *divine provision,* but that's a skimpy label for a complex theological reality. Providence is how God orchestrates everything to accomplish His purposes. Let me show you what that means by contrasting different methods God uses.

There are two ways God can act in the world: by miracle and by providence. A miracle has no natural explanation. In the flow of normal life, God suddenly stems the tide and injects a miracle. Then He sets the flow back in motion, just like parting the Red Sea until His people could walk across and then closing it up again. Do you think it would be easier to do that—to say, "Hold it, I want to do this miracle" and do it—or to say, "Let's see, I've got fifty billion circumstances to orchestrate to accomplish this one thing"? The latter is providence. Think, for example, of how God providentially ordered the lives of Joseph, Ruth, and Esther. Today He does the same for us.

Contentment comes from learning that God is sovereign not only by supernatural intervention, but also by natural orchestration. And what an incredible orchestra it is! Appreciate the complexity of what God is doing every moment just to keep us alive. When we look at things from that perspective, we see what folly it is to think we can control our lives. When we give up that vain pursuit, we give up a major source of anxiety.

Paul was content because he had confidence in the providence of God. That confidence, however, never led him to a fatalistic "It doesn't matter what I do" attitude. The example of Paul's life throughout the New Testament is this: Work as hard as you can and be content that God is in control of the results.

## SATISFACTION WITH LITTLE

Here is another secret to contentment from Paul's life: "Not that I speak from want; for I have learned to be content in whatever circumstances I am. I know how to get along with humble means, and I also know how to live in prosperity" (Phil. 4:11–12). He appreciated the revived generosity of the

Philippian church but wanted them to know he hadn't been coveting it. He kept his wants or desires in check, not confusing them with his needs.

"Not that I speak from want" is another way of saying, "I really don't have any needs that aren't being met." Our needs as human beings are simple: food, clothing, shelter, and godliness with contentment, as highlighted in our previous chapter. Scripture says to be content with the bare necessities of life.

That attitude is in marked contrast to the attitude of our culture. People today aren't content—with little or much. My theory is that the more people have, the more discontent they're apt to be. Typically, the most unhappy people you'll ever meet are very wealthy. They seem to believe their needs can never be met. Unlike Paul, they assume their wants are needs. They've followed our materialistic culture's lead in redefining human needs.

You'll never come across a commercial or ad that tells you to eat food, drink water, or go to sleep. Mass media advertise items that are far more optional and discretionary, but you'd never know it from the sales pitch. The appeal isn't "Wouldn't you like to have this?" but "You need this!" If you expose yourself to such appeals without thinking, you'll find yourself needing things you don't even want! The goal of this kind of advertising is to produce discontent and make a sale.

To protect yourself, pay careful attention to whenever you attach the word *need* to something in your thoughts or speech. Edit any use of it that goes beyond life's bare essentials. Paul did, and you can too. Thankfully regard any surplus as a blessing from God. You will be satisfied with little when you refuse to depend on luxuries the world redefines as needs.

## DETACHMENT FROM CIRCUMSTANCES

The one thing that steals our contentment more than anything else is trying circumstances. We crumble and lose our sense of satisfaction and peace when we allow our circumstances to victimize us. No doubt Paul was human and suffered that way too, but then he learned a different way: remaining content no matter what his circumstances were. "I have *learned* to be content," he said, "in whatever circumstances I am" (Phil. 4:11). He really meant *whatever*, for in the next verse he ran the gamut of extremes from great poverty to great wealth.

It's possible for us as Christians to learn to be content in facing any situation in life. And we don't have to wait for the next life to be able to do this. We do need to keep one foot in the next life, however. Paul said it this way: "Set your mind on the things above, not on the things that are on earth" (Col. 3:2). "Our light and momentary troubles are achieving for us an eternal glory that far outweighs them all. So we fix our eyes not on what is seen, but on what is unseen. For what is seen is temporary, but what is unseen is eternal" (2 Cor. 4:17–18 NIV). Paul endured many horrific circumstances (note his summary in 11:23–33), but through them he learned to be content by having an eternal perspective. Realize any circumstance you face is only temporary. The energy you're tempted to expend on it by getting anxious isn't worth being compared to your eternal reward. Learn to be content by not taking your earthly circumstances too seriously.

## BEING SUSTAINED BY DIVINE POWER

Paul could face any earthly circumstance with this confident assurance: "I can do all things through Him who strengthens me" (Phil. 4:13). He had learned that no matter how difficult things get in this material world, every Christian has a spiritual undergirding.

In saying he could do all things through Christ, Paul was referring to endurance, not miraculous provision. He didn't mean he could go on forever without eating or drinking. He couldn't be battered five thousand times and still survive. There's a limit to the physical hardships any human being can endure. Instead Paul was saying, "When I have come to the end of my own resources, then I experience the power of Christ to sustain me until a provision is made." He believed in the promise of Isaiah 40:31: "Those who wait for the LORD will gain new strength; they will mount up with wings like eagles, they will run and not get tired, they will walk and not become weary."

Contentment is a by-product of distress. It comes when you experience the sustaining power of Christ when you simply have run out of steam: "To him who lacks might He increases power" (v. 29). We do well to experience enough difficulty in our lives to see Christ's power on display in us.

I know I've grown through the years in my capacity to experience contentment. One main reason is that I've seen God do things in my life that only He could do. Otherwise I would have been prone to experience anxiety, a lack of peace, and fear of my ability to handle a difficult situation. Rather I've learned to cast myself on His strength and say, "Lord, this is a situation I cannot resolve on my own. No human resources are sufficient. I'm depending on You to see me through" (cf. 1 Cor. 10:13).

Do you know how a pacemaker works? It kicks in when the heart it's attached to doesn't work right. It's a sustaining power. We as believers have a reservoir of spiritual power that moves into action when we have come to the end of our resources. Therefore we can "do exceeding abundantly beyond all that we ask or think, according to the power that works within us" (Eph. 3:20).

You'll learn contentment when you've stood in the valley of the shadow of death, when you've been at the brink, when you can't resolve your problems, when you can't eliminate the conflict, when you can't fix your marriage, when you can't do anything about the kids, when you can't change your work environment, when you're unable to fight the disease that's wracking your body. That's when you'll turn to God and find the strength to get through the situation.

To add an important qualifier, however, if you've been living a life of sin and you're now at the bottom of the pit where sin has led you, don't expect the Lord to step in, put on a dazzling display of His power, and make you feel content. What He's more apt to do is add corrective discipline to the pain that your circumstances have naturally produced. There's no quick fix for a sinful pattern of living. Just like health is the result of right living in the physical dimension, so power from God is the result of being obedient in the spiritual dimension. A letter from a woman who experienced that speaks powerfully:

Dear John,

I cheated on my second husband for about the first eleven years of our marriage. This consisted of several short-term affairs, a couple of long-term affairs, a few one-night stands, and some miscellaneous messing around—probably twelve to fifteen men in all. I basically loved my husband, but knew I was not 100 percent committed to him and had no idea how to change that.

I was miserable. I had no sense of self-worth, was very moody, discontent, and shopped a lot to try to satisfy my emptiness. However, I was a very adept liar and managed to deceive my husband as well as everyone else. I was still able to function pretty well most of the time in spite of all this, and most people actually thought I was a good person because I hid the bad side of me so well. I put on a very good front for most of the world to see, but I felt like I had on a mask all the time. If anyone ever told me I was attractive, I would think to myself, If you could only see what's inside of me, you wouldn't say that!

I guess I should also mention I had an abortion, a baby conceived by my second husband while I was still married to my first. We separated, I had the abortion, then married my present husband one-and-a-half years after living with him most of the time.

Because of recurring depression I went for counseling. After two years of it I better understood some of my reasons for doing what I did, but in no way did I change. My background is that of a Christian home. In fact, my father was a minister and I "accepted Christ" at an early age. I really never understood what it was to follow Christ, however. I went through a lot of the motions as I was growing up, but it didn't mean much to me. As soon as I left home to go to college, I rejected everything and went on my merry way. My heart was very cold to the things of God, and I'm sure Satan was happy to oblige by hardening it even more.

Maybe two or three times in my deepest depression and despair I cried out for God to help me, but I didn't bother to say I was sorry for what I was doing. And since I never heard from Him, I was totally convinced He hated me and didn't want to have anything to do with me ever again. This added to my misery and feelings of worthlessness.

Yet I am living proof of the Holy Spirit's power to transform a person's heart and behavior. Not all convictions for a changed life came at once. It's been a gradual process for certain things, but one thing did change immediately because I believe God knew it was most important to me: the thought of ever being with another man simply abhors me. I realized that I was committed to my unsaved husband and my marriage 100 percent, and that I loved him with all my heart and would never do anything again to dishonor him. This was not something I had specifically asked for—it just happened! I had a deep feeling of joy and contentment, a word I thought I would never know the meaning of in my lifetime.

Once this woman turned to God in obedient faith, He wonderfully blessed her with spiritual power and contentment.

The same blessings await any other obedient believer who has
come to the end of his or her resources.

## PREOCCUPATION WITH THE WELL-BEING OF OTHERS

If you live for yourself, you will never be content. Many of us
don't experience contentment because we demand our world
to be exactly the way we want it to be. We want our spouse
to fulfill our expectations and agenda. We want our children
to conform to a prewritten plan we have ordained for them
to fulfill. And we want everything else to fall into its perfect
niche in the little cupboard where we compartmentalize
every element of existence.

Paul prayed for the Philippians to have a different perspective. He began his letter to them with a prayer that their
love for one another might be abundant (Phil. 1:9) and went
on to give this practical advice: "Do nothing from selfishness
or empty conceit, but with humility of mind let each of you
regard one another as more important than himself" (Phil.
2:3). He wanted them to lose themselves by being preoccupied with the well-being of others. This was the example he
gave to them and us:

> Nevertheless, you have done well to share with
> me in my affliction. And you yourselves also
> know, Philippians, that at the first preaching of
> the gospel, after I departed from Macedonia, no
> church shared with me in the matter of giving and
> receiving but you alone; for even in Thessalonica
> you sent a gift more than once for my needs. Not
> that I seek the gift itself, but I seek for the profit

which increases to your account. But I have received everything in full, and have an abundance; I am amply supplied, having received from Epaphroditus what you have sent, a fragrant aroma, an acceptable sacrifice, well pleasing to God. And my God shall supply all your needs according to His riches in glory in Christ Jesus. (Phil. 4:14–19)

Even though Paul was assured of God's providence, independent of his circumstances, and strengthened by divine power, he knew how to write a gracious thank-you note. He wanted the Philippians to know they had done a noble thing in caring for his needs. They were a poor church from Macedonia (an area whose poverty is described in 2 Cor. 8—9) that had apparently sent food, clothing, and money to Paul in Rome through Epaphroditus. Their generosity impressed Paul.

Notice what made him happiest of all about the gift: "Not that I seek the gift itself, but I seek for the profit which increases to your account" (Phil. 4:17). He was more interested in their spiritual benefit than his material gain. Being comfortable, well fed, and satisfied weren't Paul's main concerns in life. Rather, he was interested in accruing eternal dividends to the lives of the people he loved. Here are the timeless scriptural principles that apply:

- Proverbs 11:24–25: "There is one who scatters, yet increases all the more, and there is one who withholds what is justly due, but it results only in want. The generous man will be prosperous, and he who waters will himself be watered."

- Proverbs 19:17: "He who is gracious to a poor man lends to the LORD, and He will repay him for his good deed."
- Luke 6:38: "Give, and it will be given to you."
- 2 Corinthians 9:6: "He who sows sparingly shall also reap sparingly; and he who sows bountifully shall also reap bountifully."

Paul described the gift he had received as "a fragrant aroma, an acceptable sacrifice, well pleasing to God" (Phil. 4:18). He was using Old Testament imagery to say, "Not only did you give it to me, but you also gave it to God." At the beginning of our passage, in verse 10, we noted how happy Paul was to receive the gift. His joy came not because he finally received what he had been wanting (as we saw in verse 11, he politely mentioned that he didn't need it), but because the Philippians had given him something that honored God and would accrue to their spiritual benefit.

Their doing that led Paul to say in closing, "My God shall supply all your needs according to His riches in glory in Christ Jesus" (v. 19). That is one of the most often-quoted verses of Scripture, but it needs to be set in its context. Paul was saying, "You gave to me in a way that left you in need. I want to assure you that God will not remain in your debt. He will supply all your needs." It refers to material, earthly needs sacrificed by the Philippians that God in response to their sacrifice would amply replenish.

If you likewise "honor the LORD from your wealth … your barns will be filled with plenty, and your vats will overflow with new wine" (Prov. 3:9–10). God's not going to give you back spiritual blessings only and let you die of hunger. If you're in Christ, the riches of God in glory are yours. That is why, as we learned in our first chapter, we are not to be preoccupied with what we eat, drink, or wear. Instead we are to "seek first His kingdom, and His righteousness; and … not be anxious" (Matt. 6:33–34).

Attack anxiety in your life by applying what you have learned about contentment. Be confident in God's sovereign providence, and don't allow your circumstances to trouble you. Instead of giving in to panic, cling to the promise of Romans 8:28: "We know that God causes all things to work together for good to those who love God." Regard that verse as a spiritual lifeline for the rest of your life. Also, buck the tide of our materialistic, selfish society by being satisfied with little and more concerned about the spiritual welfare of others than your material needs. Be obedient to God's Word and confident in His power to meet all your needs. May our Lord keep all these principles in the forefront of our minds that we might be content—and free from anxiety!

Be more concerned with the
Spiritual welfare of others than
my own material needs.
Be obedient to God's word and
Confident in His power to meet all
your needs.

# APPENDIX:
# PSALMS FOR THE ANXIOUS

ॐ

These excerpts from the Psalms are especially intended to attack anxiety. They movingly express and offer counsel in dealing with anxious thoughts and feelings we *all* have experienced. To derive the most benefit from this collection, you may want to scan them in one sitting and put a pencil mark by the ones you more closely relate to. Go back and carefully read all the ones you marked, perhaps from several different Bible versions. Out of those, select the ones that minister to you the most, and over time examine them in their entire context. To help you in your in-depth study, have on hand a good commentary on the Psalms, such as Charles Spurgeon's *The Treasury of David,* 3 vols. (McLean, VA: Macdonald, n.d.).

## PSALM 3:

You are a shield around me, O LORD; you bestow glory on me and lift up my head. *To the LORD, I cry aloud,* and *he answers me* from his holy hill. *I lie down and sleep; I wake again, because the LORD sustains me. I will not fear....* Arise, O LORD! Deliver me, O my God! (vv. 3–7 NIV)

## PSALM 4:

Answer me when I call, O God of my righteousness! *Thou hast relieved me in my distress;* be gracious to me and hear my prayer.... But know that the LORD has set apart the godly man for Himself; the LORD hears when I call to Him. Tremble, and do not sin; meditate in your heart upon your bed, and be still. Offer the sacrifices of righteousness, and trust in the LORD. Many are saying, "Who will show us any good?" Lift up the light of Thy countenance upon us, O LORD! Thou hast put gladness in my heart, more than when their grain and new wine abound. *In peace I will both lie down and sleep,* for Thou alone, O LORD, dost make me to dwell in safety. (vv. 1, 3–8)

## PSALM 5:

Give ear to my words, O LORD, consider my meditation. *Hearken unto the voice of my cry,* my King, and my God: for unto thee will I pray. My voice shalt thou hear in the morning, O LORD; in the morning will I direct my prayer unto thee, and will look up.... *Let all those that put their trust in thee rejoice:* let them ever shout for joy, because thou defendest them: let them also that love thy name be joyful in thee.

For thou, LORD, wilt bless the righteous; with favor wilt thou compass him as with a shield. (vv. 1–3, 11–12 KJV)

## PSALM 6:

No, Lord! Don't punish me in the heat of your anger. Pity me, O Lord, for I am weak. Heal me, for my body is sick, and *I am upset and disturbed.* My mind is filled with apprehension and with gloom. Oh, restore me soon…. I am worn out with pain; every night my pillow is wet with tears. My eyes are growing old and dim with grief…. Go, leave me now, you men of evil deeds, for the Lord has heard my weeping and my pleading. He will answer all my prayers. (vv. 1–3, 6–9 TLB)

## PSALM 7:

O LORD my God, *I take refuge in you;* save and deliver me…. My shield is God Most High, who saves the upright in heart…. I will give thanks to the LORD because of his righteousness and will sing praise to the name of the LORD Most High. (vv. 1, 10, 17 NIV)

## PSALM 8:

O LORD, our Lord, how excellent is thy name in all the earth! who hast set thy glory above the heavens…. When I consider thy heavens, the work of thy fingers, the moon and the stars, which thou hast ordained; *what is man, that thou art mindful of him?* and the son of man, that thou visitest him? For thou hast made him a little lower than the angels, and hast crowned him with glory and honour. Thou madest him to have dominion over the works of thy hands; thou hast put all things under his feet. (vv. 1, 3–6 KJV)

## PSALM 9:

I will give thanks to the LORD with all my heart; I will tell of all Thy wonders. I will be glad and exult in Thee; I will sing praise to Thy name, O Most High.... For Thou hast maintained my just cause; Thou dost sit on the throne judging righteously.... The LORD ... will execute judgment for the peoples with equity. *The LORD* also *will be* a stronghold for the oppressed, *a stronghold in times of trouble,* and those who know Thy name will put their trust in Thee; for *Thou, O LORD, hast not forsaken those who seek Thee.* (vv. 1–2, 4, 7–10)

## PSALM 10:

*Why, O LORD, do you stand far off?* Why do you hide yourself in times of trouble? ... But you, O God, do see trouble and grief; you consider it to take it in hand. The victim commits himself to you; you are the helper of the fatherless. (vv. 1, 14 NIV)

## PSALM 11:

*In the LORD I take refuge.* How then can you say to me: "Flee like a bird to your mountain.... When the foundations are being destroyed, what can the righteous do?" (vv. 1, 3 NIV)

## PSALM 13:

How long will you forget me, Lord? Forever? How long will you look the other way when I am in need? *How long must I be hiding daily anguish in my heart?* How long shall my enemy have the upper hand? Answer me, O Lord my God; give me light in my darkness lest I die.... *But I will always trust in you* and in your mercy and shall rejoice in your salvation. I will sing to the Lord because he has blessed me so richly. (vv. 1–3, 5–6 TLB)

## PSALM 16:

*Keep me safe, O God,* for in you I take refuge. I said to the LORD, "You are my Lord; apart from you I have no good thing." ... LORD, you have assigned me my portion and my cup; you have made my lot secure.... I will praise the LORD, who counsels me; even at night my heart instructs me. *I have set the LORD always before me. Because he is at my right hand, I will not be shaken.* Therefore my heart is glad and my tongue rejoices; my body also will rest secure.... You have made known to me the path of life; you will fill me with joy in your presence, with eternal pleasures. (vv. 1–2, 5, 7–9, 11 NIV)

## PSALM 18:

I love Thee, O LORD, my strength. The LORD is my rock and my fortress and my deliverer, my God, my rock, in whom I take refuge.... *The cords of death encompassed me,* and the torrents of ungodliness terrified me.... In my distress I called upon the LORD, and ... my cry for help ... came into His ears.... He sent from on high, He took me; He drew me out of many waters.... He brought me forth also into a [spacious] place; He rescued me, because He delighted in me.... Thou dost light my lamp; *the LORD my God illumines my darkness.* For by Thee I can run upon a troop; and by my God I can leap over a wall. As for God, His way is blameless; the word of the LORD is [flawless].... *He is a shield to all who take refuge in Him....* He makes my feet like hinds' feet, and sets me upon my high places.... The LORD lives, and blessed be my rock; and exalted be the God of my salvation. (vv. 1–2, 4, 6, 16, 19, 28–30, 33, 46)

## PSALM 19:

*The law of the LORD is perfect, reviving the soul....* The precepts of the LORD are right, giving joy to the heart.... May the words of my mouth and the meditation of my heart be pleasing in your sight, O LORD, my Rock and my Redeemer. (vv. 7–8, 14 NIV)

## PSALM 22:

*My God, my God, why have you forsaken me?* Why do you refuse to help me or even to listen to my groans? Day and night I keep on weeping, crying for your help, but there is no reply.... The praises of our fathers surrounded your throne; they trusted you and you delivered them. You heard their cries for help and saved them; they were never disappointed when they sought your aid.... O Lord, don't stay away. O God my Strength, hurry to my aid. Rescue me from death; spare my precious life.... I will stand up before the congregation and testify of the wonderful things you have done.... I will say[, "H]e has not despised my cries of deep despair; he has not turned and walked away. When I cried to him, he heard and came." (vv. 1–5, 19–20, 22–24 TLB)

## PSALM 23:

*The LORD is my shepherd;* I shall not want. He maketh me to lie down in green pastures: he leadeth me beside the still waters.

*He restoreth my soul:* he leadeth me in the paths of righteousness for his name's sake. Yea, though I walk through the valley of the shadow of death, I will fear no evil: for thou art with me; *thy rod and thy staff they comfort me....* Surely goodness and mercy shall follow me all the days of my life: and I will dwell in the house of the LORD for ever. (vv. 1–4, 6 KJV)

## PSALM 25:

To Thee, O LORD, I lift up my soul. O my God, in Thee I trust, do not let me be ashamed.... Indeed, none of those who wait for Thee will be ashamed.... Make me know Thy ways, O LORD; teach me Thy paths. Lead me in Thy truth and teach me, for Thou art the God of my salvation; for Thee I wait all the day.... Do not remember the sins of my youth or my transgressions; according to Thy lovingkindness remember Thou me, for Thy goodness' sake, O LORD.... My eyes are continually toward the LORD, for He will pluck my feet out of the net. *Turn to me and be gracious to me, for I am lonely and afflicted.* The troubles of my heart are enlarged; *bring me out of my distresses.* Look upon my affliction and my trouble.... Guard my soul and deliver me ... for I take refuge in Thee. (vv. 1–5, 7, 15–18, 20)

## PSALM 27:

Wait on the LORD: be of good courage, and *he shall strengthen thine heart.* (v. 14 KJV)

## PSALM 28:

To you I call, O LORD my Rock; *do not turn a deaf ear to me....* Praise be to the LORD, for he has heard my cry for mercy. The

LORD is my strength and my shield; *my heart trusts in him, and I am helped.* My heart leaps for joy and I will give thanks to him in song. (vv. 1, 6–7 NIV)

## PSALM 30:

I will extol Thee, O LORD, for Thou hast lifted me up ... O LORD my God, I cried to Thee for help, and Thou didst heal me. O LORD, Thou hast brought up my soul from [the grave]; Thou hast kept me alive, that I should not go down to the pit.... *Weeping may last for the night, but a shout of joy comes in the morning.* Now as for me, I said ... "I will never be moved." O LORD, by Thy favor Thou hast made my mountain to stand strong.... *Thou hast turned for me my mourning into dancing* ... that my soul may sing praise to Thee, and not be silent. O LORD my God, I will give thanks to Thee forever. (vv. 1–3, 5–7, 11–12)

## PSALM 31:

In you, O LORD, I have taken refuge; let me never be put to shame.... Turn your ear to me, come quickly to my rescue; be my rock of refuge, a strong fortress to save me.... Into your hands I commit my spirit.... I will be glad and rejoice in your love, for *you saw my affliction and knew the anguish of my soul.*... Be merciful to me, O LORD, for I am in distress; my eyes grow weak with sorrow, my soul and my body with grief. My life is consumed by anguish and my years by groaning; my strength fails because of my affliction, and my bones grow weak.... But I trust in you, O LORD; I say, "You are my God." *My times are in your hands.*... Be strong and take heart, all you who hope in the LORD. (vv. 1–2, 5, 7, 9–10, 14–15, 24 NIV)

## PSALM 32:

When I kept silent about my sin, my body wasted away through my groaning all day long. *For day and night Thy hand was heavy upon me;* my vitality was drained away as with the fever-heat of summer. I acknowledged my sin to Thee, and my iniquity I did not hide; I said, "I will confess my transgressions to the LORD"; and Thou didst forgive the guilt of my sin. Therefore, let everyone who is godly pray to Thee.... Surely ... a flood of great waters ... shall not reach him. *Thou art my hiding place;* Thou dost preserve me from trouble; Thou dost surround me with songs of deliverance. (vv. 3–7)

## PSALM 34:

I sought the LORD, and he answered me; *he delivered me from all my fears. Those who look to him are radiant;* their faces are never covered with shame. This poor man called, and the LORD heard him; he saved him out of all his troubles. The angel of the LORD encamps around those who fear him, and he delivers them.... The righteous cry out, and the LORD hears them; he delivers them from all their troubles. *The LORD is close to the brokenhearted and saves those who are crushed in spirit. A righteous man may have many troubles, but the LORD delivers him from them all.* (vv. 4–7, 17–19 NIV)

## PSALM 37:

*Do not fret....* Trust in the LORD and do good.... Delight yourself in the LORD and he will give you the desires of your heart. Commit your way to the LORD; trust in him and he will ... make your righteousness shine like the dawn, the justice of your cause like the noonday sun. Be still before the LORD and wait patiently for him.... *Do not fret—it leads only to evil....* The LORD upholds the righteous ... [whose steps he has made] firm; though he stumble, he will not fall, for the LORD upholds him with his hand.... The LORD loves the just and will not forsake his faithful ones.... He is their stronghold in time of trouble. (vv. 1, 3–8, 17, 23–24, 28, 39 NIV)

## PSALM 38:

I am benumbed and badly crushed; I groan because of the agitation of my heart. Lord, all my desire is before Thee; and my sighing is not hidden from Thee.... I am ready to fall, and my sorrow is continually before me. For I confess my iniquity; *I am full of anxiety* because of my sin.... Do not forsake me.... O my God, do not be far from me! *Make haste to help me, O Lord,* my salvation! (vv. 8–9, 17–18, 21–22)

## PSALM 40:

I waited patiently for the LORD; he turned to me and heard my cry. *He lifted me out of the slimy pit, out of the mud and mire;* he set my feet on a rock and gave me a firm place to stand. *He put a new song in my mouth,* a hymn of praise to our God. Many will see and fear and put their trust in the LORD. (vv. 1–3 NIV)

## PSALM 42:

*Why are you downcast, O my soul? Why so disturbed within me?* Put your hope in God, for I will yet praise him, my Savior and my God. My soul is downcast within me; therefore I will remember you. (vv. 5–6; cf. 42:11; 43:5 NIV)

### PSALM 46:

*God is our refuge and strength, a very present help in trouble.* Therefore will not we fear, though the earth be removed.... Be still, and know that I am God. (vv. 1–2, 10 KJV)

### PSALM 48:

Great is the LORD, and most worthy of praise.... For this God is our God forever and ever; *he will be our guide even to the end.* (vv. 1, 14 NIV)

### PSALM 54:

Save me, O God, by your name; vindicate me by your might. Hear my prayer, O God; listen to the words of my mouth.... *Surely God is my help; the Lord is the one who sustains me....* For he has delivered me from all my troubles. (vv. 1–2, 4, 7 NIV)

### PSALM 55:

Give ear to my prayer, O God; and do not hide Thyself from my supplication. Give heed to me, and answer me; I am restless in my complaint and am surely distracted.... My heart is in anguish within me, and the terrors of death have fallen upon me. *Fear and trembling come upon me; and horror has overwhelmed me....* I said, "O that I had wings like a dove! I would fly away and be at rest.... I would wander far away ... from the stormy wind and tempest." ... I shall call upon God, and the LORD will save me.... *Cast your burden upon the LORD, and He will sustain you;* He will never allow the righteous to be shaken.... I will trust in Thee. (vv. 1–2, 4–8, 16, 22–23)

### PSALM 56:

When I am afraid, I will trust in you. In God, whose word I praise, *in God I trust; I will not be afraid....* You have delivered me from death and my feet from stumbling, that I may walk before God in the light of life. (vv. 3–4, 13 NIV)

### PSALM 57:

Have mercy on me, O God, have mercy on me, for in you my soul takes refuge. *I will take refuge in the shadow of your wings until the disaster has passed.* I cry out to God Most High, to God, who fulfills his purpose for me.... My heart is steadfast, O God, ... I will sing and make music.... For great is your love, reaching to the heavens; your faithfulness reaches to the skies. (vv. 1–2, 7, 10 NIV)

### PSALM 61:

Hear my cry, O God; attend unto my prayer. From the end of the earth will I cry unto thee, when my heart is overwhelmed: *lead me to the rock that is higher than I.* (vv. 1–2 KJV)

### PSALM 62:

*My soul finds rest in God alone;* my salvation comes from him. He alone is my rock and my salvation; he is my fortress, I will never be shaken. (vv. 1–2 NIV)

### PSALM 63:

O God, you are my God, earnestly I seek you; my soul thirsts for you, my body longs for you, in a dry and weary land where there is no water.... On my bed I remember you; *I think of you through the watches of the night.* Because you are my help, I sing in the shadow of your wings. *My soul clings to you;* your right hand upholds me. (vv. 1, 6–8 NIV)

## PSALM 68:

Praise be to the Lord, to God our Savior, who daily bears our burdens. Our God is a God who saves; from the Sovereign LORD comes escape from death. (vv. 19–20 NIV)

## PSALM 69:

Save me, O God, for the waters have come up to my soul. I have sunk in deep mire, and there is no foothold; I have come into deep waters, and a flood overflows me. *I am weary with my crying;* my throat is parched; my eyes fail while I wait for my God.... O God, it is Thou who dost know my folly, and my wrongs are not hidden from Thee. May those who wait for Thee not be ashamed through me.... But as for me, my prayer is to Thee.... Deliver me from the mire, and *do not let me sink....* According to the greatness of Thy compassion, turn to me, and do not hide Thy face from Thy servant, for I am in distress; *answer me quickly.... I looked* for sympathy, but there was none; *and for comforters, but I found none....* I am afflicted and in pain; *may Thy salvation, O God, set me securely on high.* I will praise the name of God with song, and shall magnify Him with thanksgiving.... For the LORD hears the needy, and does not despise His who are prisoners. (vv. 1–3, 5–6, 13–14, 16–17, 20, 29–30, 33)

## PSALM 70:

Make haste, O God, to deliver me; *make haste to help me, O Lord*.... Let all those that seek thee rejoice and be glad in thee: and let such as love thy salvation say continually, Let God be magnified. (vv. 1, 4 KJV)

## PSALM 71:

In Thee, O LORD, I have taken refuge; let me never be ashamed. In Thy righteousness deliver me, and rescue me; incline Thine ear to me, and save me. Be Thou to me a rock of habitation, to which I may continually come; Thou hast given commandment to save me, for Thou art my rock and my fortress.... I will hope continually, and will praise Thee yet more and more. My mouth shall tell of Thy righteousness, and of Thy salvation all day long.... Even when I am old and gray, O God, do not forsake me, until I declare Thy strength to this generation, Thy power to all who are to come.... *Thou, who hast showed me many troubles and distresses, wilt revive me again* ... and turn to comfort me. (vv. 1–3, 14–15, 18, 20–21)

## PSALM 73:

When *my heart was grieved and my spirit embittered*, I was senseless and ignorant; I was a brute beast before you. *Yet* I am always with you; *you hold me* by my right hand. *You guide me with your counsel*, and afterward you will take me into glory. Whom have I in heaven but you? And earth has nothing I desire besides you. My flesh and my heart may fail, but God is the strength of my heart and my portion forever. (vv. 21–26 NIV)

## PSALM 77:

My voice rises to God, and I will cry aloud; my voice rises to God, and He will hear me. In the day of my trouble I sought the Lord; in the night my hand was stretched out without weariness; *my soul refused to be comforted*.... Thou hast held my eyelids open; *I am so troubled that I cannot speak.* I have considered the ... years of long ago.... My spirit ponders.... Has God forgotten to be gracious? Or has He in anger withdrawn His compassion? ... I shall remember the deeds of the LORD.... I will meditate on all Thy work, and muse on Thy deeds. Thy way, O God, is holy; what god is great like our God? ... Thou hast by Thy power redeemed Thy people. (vv. 1–2, 4–6, 9, 11–13, 15)

## PSALM 84:

Blessed are those whose strength is in you, who have set their hearts on pilgrimage.... They go from strength to strength, till each appears before God.... *The LORD God is a sun and shield;* the LORD bestows favor and honor; no good thing does he withhold from those whose walk is blameless. O LORD Almighty, blessed is the man who trusts in you. (vv. 5, 7, 11–12 NIV)

## PSALM 86:

Hear, O LORD, and answer me, for *I am poor and needy.* Guard my life, for I am devoted to you. You are my God; save your servant who trusts in you. Have mercy on me, O Lord, for *I call to you all day long.* Bring joy to your servant, for to you, O Lord, I lift up my soul. (vv. 1–4 NIV)

### PSALM 89:

*Blessed are those who have learned to acclaim you,* who walk in the light of your presence, O LORD. They rejoice in your name all day long; they exult in your righteousness. For you are their glory and strength. (vv. 15–17 NIV)

### PSALM 90:

*Relent, O LORD! How long will it be?* Have compassion on your servants. Satisfy us in the morning with your unfailing love, that we may sing for joy and be glad all our days. *Make us glad for as many days as you have afflicted us,* for as many years as we have seen trouble.... May the favor of the Lord our God rest upon us; establish the work of our hands for us—yes, establish the work of our hands. (vv. 13–15, 17 NIV)

### PSALM 91:

He who dwells in the shelter of the Most High will rest in the shadow of the Almighty. I will say of the LORD, "He is my refuge and my fortress, my God, in whom I trust." ... *"Because he loves me," says the LORD, "I will rescue him;* I will protect him, for he acknowledges my name. He will call upon me, and I will answer him; I will be with him in trouble, I will deliver him and honor him." (vv. 1–2, 14–15, NIV)

### PSALM 94:

When I said, "My foot is slipping," your love, O LORD, supported me. *When anxiety was great within me, your consolation brought joy to my soul....* The LORD has become my fortress, and my God the rock in whom I take refuge. (vv. 18–19, 22 NIV)

### PSALM 100:

Serve the LORD with gladness: come before his presence with singing.... For *the LORD is good; his mercy is everlasting;* and his truth endureth to all generations. (vv. 2, 5 KJV)

### PSALM 102:

Hear my prayer, O LORD; let my cry for help come to you. Do not hide your face from me when I am in distress. Turn your ear to me; when I call, answer me quickly.... *My heart is blighted and withered like grass; I forget to eat my food.* Because of my loud groaning I am reduced to skin and bones.... I lie awake ... because of your great wrath, for you have taken me up and thrown me aside.... [But the Lord] will respond to the prayer of the destitute; he will not despise their plea. (vv. 1–2, 4–5, 7, 10, 17 NIV)

### PSALM 103:

The LORD is compassionate and gracious, slow to anger and abounding in lovingkindness. He will not always strive with us; nor will He keep His anger forever. He has not dealt with us according to our sins, nor rewarded us according to our iniquities. For *high as the heavens are above the earth, so great is His lovingkindness toward those who fear Him....* Just as a father has compassion on his children, so the LORD has compassion on those who fear Him. For He Himself knows our frame; *He is mindful that we are but dust.* (vv. 8–11, 13–14)

## Psalm 107:

*Some sat in darkness and the deepest gloom* ... for they had rebelled against the words of God.... Then they cried to the Lord in their trouble, and he saved them from their distress.... Some became fools through their rebellious ways and suffered affliction because of their iniquities ... and drew near the gates of death. *Then they cried to the Lord in their trouble, and he saved them from their distress.* He sent forth his word and healed them; he rescued them from the grave. Let them give thanks to the Lord for his unfailing love and his wonderful deeds for men.... He lifted the needy out of their affliction.... Whoever is wise, let him heed these things and consider the great love of the Lord. (vv. 10–11, 13, 17–21, 41, 43 NIV)

## Psalm 112:

Blessed is the man who fears the Lord, who finds great delight in his commands.... Surely he will never be shaken; a righteous man will be remembered forever. *He will have no fear of bad news; his heart is steadfast,* trusting in the Lord. His heart is secure, he will have no fear. (vv. 1, 6–8 NIV)

## Psalm 116:

*I love the Lord, because He hears my voice* and my supplications.... Therefore I shall call upon Him as long as I live. The cords of death encompassed me.... I found distress and sorrow.... *I was brought low, and He saved me.* Return to your rest, O my soul, for the Lord has dealt bountifully with you.... Thou hast rescued my soul from death, my eyes from tears, my feet from stumbling. I shall walk before the LORD in the land of the living. (vv. 1–3, 6–9)

## PSALM 118:

From my distress I called upon the LORD; the LORD answered me and set me in a large place. *The LORD is for me; I will not fear; what can man do to me?* ... It is better to take refuge in the LORD than to trust in man.... You pushed me violently so that I was falling, but the LORD helped me. The LORD is my strength and song, and He has become my salvation.... I shall not die, but live, and tell of the works of the LORD. *The LORD has disciplined me severely, but He has not given me over to death.* (vv. 5–6, 8, 13–14, 17–18)

## PSALM 119:

*I am laid low in the dust; preserve my life according to your word....* My soul is weary with sorrow; strengthen me according to your word.... My comfort in my suffering is this: Your promise preserves my life.... Before I was afflicted I went astray, but now I obey your word. *You are good, and what you do is good.... It was good for me to be afflicted so that I might learn your decrees....* My soul faints with longing for your salvation, but I have put my hope in your word. My eyes fail, looking for your promise; I say, "When will you comfort me?" ... If your law had not been my delight, I would have perished in my affliction.... I have suffered much; preserve my life, O LORD, according to your word.... Trouble and distress have come upon me, but your commands are my delight.... *Great peace have they who love your law, and nothing can make them stumble.* (vv. 25, 28, 50, 67–68, 71, 81–82, 92, 107, 143, 165 NIV)

### PSALM 120:

*I call on the LORD in my distress,* and he answers me. (v. 1 NIV)

### PSALM 121:

*I will lift up mine eyes unto the hills, from whence cometh my help. My help cometh from the LORD,* [who] made heaven and earth.... *He will not let your foot slip....* The LORD watches over you.... [He] will keep you from all harm—he will watch over your life; the LORD will watch over your coming and going both now and forevermore. (vv. 1–2 KJV; vv. 3, 5, 7–8 NIV)

### PSALM 123:

As the eyes of servants look unto the hand of their masters ... so *our eyes wait upon the LORD our God,* until that he have mercy upon us. (v. 2 KJV)

### PSALM 126:

*He who goes out weeping,* carrying seed to sow, *will return with songs of joy,* carrying sheaves with him. (v. 6 NIV)

### PSALM 130:

*Out of the depths I cry to you, O LORD....* Let your ears be attentive to my cry for mercy. If you, O LORD, kept a record of sins ... who could stand? But with you there is forgiveness.... *I wait for the LORD,* my soul waits, *and in his word I put my hope.* (vv. 1–5 NIV)

## Psalm 131:

O Lord, my heart is not proud, or my eyes haughty; nor do I involve myself in great matters, or in things too difficult for me. *Surely I have composed and quieted my soul....* My soul is like a weaned child within me.... *Hope in the Lord from this time forth and forever.* (vv. 1–3)

## Psalm 138:

When I called, you answered me; you made me bold and stouthearted.... Though the Lord is on high, he looks upon the lowly.... *Though I walk in the midst of trouble, you preserve my life....* The Lord will fulfill his purpose for me; your love, O Lord, endures forever. (vv. 3, 6–8 NIV)

## Psalm 139:

O Lord, you have searched me and you know me.... You perceive my thoughts from afar.... You are familiar with all my ways. Before a word is on my tongue you know it completely, O Lord.... Where can I go from your Spirit? Where can I flee from your presence? ... If I rise on the wings of the dawn, if I settle on the far side of the sea, even there your hand will guide me, your right hand will hold me fast.... You created my inmost being.... I praise you because I am fearfully and wonderfully made; your works are wonderful, I know that full well.... All the days ordained for me were written in your book before one of them came to be.... *Search me, O God, and know my heart; test me and know my anxious thoughts.* See if there is any offensive way in me, and lead me in the way everlasting. (vv. 1–4, 7, 9–10, 13–14, 16, 23–24 NIV)

### PSALM 142:

How I plead with God, how I implore his mercy, pouring out my troubles before him. For *I am overwhelmed and desperate,* and you alone know which way I ought to turn. (vv. 1–3 TLB)

### PSALM 143:

My spirit is overwhelmed within me; *my heart is appalled within me.* I remember the days of old; I meditate on all Thy doings; I muse on the work of Thy hands. I stretch out my hands to Thee; my soul longs for Thee, as a parched land.... Let me hear Thy lovingkindness in the morning; for I trust in Thee; *teach me the way in which I should walk;* for to Thee I lift up my soul.... I take refuge in Thee. Teach me to do Thy will, for Thou art my God; *let Thy good Spirit lead me on level ground.* (vv. 4–6, 8–10)

### PSALM 145:

*The* LORD upholds all those who fall and *lifts up all who are bowed down.* The eyes of all look to you, and you give them their food at the proper time.... The LORD is near ... to all who call on him in truth. (vv. 14–15, 18 NIV)

### PSALM 146:

Praise the LORD, O my soul. I will praise the LORD all my life; *I will sing praise to my God as long as I live.* (vv. 1–2 NIV)

## PSALM 147:

How good it is to sing praises to our God, how pleasant and fitting to praise him! ... *He heals the brokenhearted and binds up their wounds....* Great is our Lord and mighty in power; his understanding has no limit. The LORD sustains the humble.... [He] delights in those who ... put their hope in his unfailing love. (vv. 1, 3, 5–6, 11 NIV)

# READERS' GUIDE

*for Personal Reflection or
Group Discussion*

# READERS' GUIDE

༄

Before beginning your personal or group study of *Anxious for Nothing*, take time to read these introductory comments.

If you are working through the study on your own, you may want to adapt certain sections (for example, the icebreakers) and record your responses to all questions in a separate notebook. You might find it more enriching or motivating to study with a partner with whom you can share answers or insights.

If you are leading a group, you may want to ask your group members to read each assigned chapter and work through the study questions before the group meets. This isn't always easy for busy adults, so encourage them with occasional phone calls or notes between meetings. Help members manage their time by suggesting that they identify a regular time of the day or week that they can devote to the study. They too may want to write their responses to the questions in a notebook. To help keep group discussion focused on the material in *Anxious for Nothing*, it is important that each member have his or her own copy of the book.

Notice that each session includes the following features:

**Chapter Theme**—a brief statement summarizing the chapter.

**Icebreakers**—activities to help each member get better acquainted with the session topic or with each other.

**Group Discovery Questions**—a list of questions to encourage individual discovery or group participation.

**Personal Application Questions**—an aid to applying the knowledge gained through study to one's personal living (Note: These are important questions for group members to answer for themselves, even if they do not wish to discuss their responses in the meeting.)

**Focus on Prayer**—suggestions for turning one's learning into prayer.

**Assignment**—an activity to complete or preparation for the next session.

Here are a few tips that can help you more effectively lead small-group studies:

**Pray** for each group member, asking the Lord to help you create an open atmosphere where everyone will feel free to share with one another and you.

**Encourage** group members to bring their Bibles as well as their texts to each session. This book is based on the New American Standard Bible, but it is good to have several translations on hand for purposes of comparison.

**Start** and end on time. This is especially important for the first meeting because it will set the pattern for the rest of the sessions.

**Begin** with prayer, asking the Holy Spirit to open hearts and minds and to give understanding so that truth will be applied.

**Involve** everyone. As learners, we retain only 10 percent of what we hear; 20 percent of what we see; 65 percent of what we hear and see; but 90 percent of what we hear, see, and do.

**Promote** a relaxed environment. Arrange the chairs in a circle or semicircle. This allows eye contact among members and encourages dynamic discussion. Be relaxed in your own attitude and manner. Be willing to share yourself.

## CHAPTER 1
## OBSERVING HOW GOD CARES FOR YOU

### CHAPTER THEME

In Matthew 6:25–34 Jesus said not to be anxious because of the abundant evidence all around us of God's lavish care for the needs of His beloved.

### ICEBREAKERS

1. Suppose you are Sherlock Holmes talking with Dr. John Watson about being a keener observer. Explain to him the logic of what Jesus says about observation in Matthew 6:25–34.
2. If you were walking with a little child on a beautiful spring day, what things might you point out to illustrate God's bountiful provision for the world's needs?

### GROUP DISCOVERY QUESTIONS

1. What kind of order is Jesus issuing in Matthew 6:25–34?
2. Explain the etymology of the English word *worry*.
3. If you are going to worry, is it somewhat acceptable if, at least, it's about the basics of life instead of about luxuries? Why or why not?
4. Does having a savings account or owning insurance imply a lack of trust in God? Explain your answer.

5. Explain how knowing what God is like relates to our concerns about the basics of life.

6. What does thinking about birds tell you about how to conduct your life?

7. Is the world facing starvation? Explain how the U.S. Department of Agriculture answers that question, then how that relates to worry.

8. How can you experience life to the fullest—no matter how long or short its span?

9. What does God's lavishing such incredible beauty on temporary wildflowers tell us about His provision for His children?

10. Explain, in relation to anxiety, the concept of believing God for the greater gift but not for the lesser one.

11. How does worry paralyze its victim?

12. Explain what Jay Adams says about tomorrow belonging to God.

13. How does seeking God's kingdom as your first priority relate to anxiety?

## Personal Application Questions

1. What is your heart's preoccupation? Are you more concerned with the kingdom or with the things of this world? Think carefully and be honest with yourself. To help you in your evaluation, make a list of the different things you do during the week. Next to each item, note whether that

time is spent for you or for God. How do you spend the majority of your time? Do you need to spend more of your time concentrating on heavenly things? Take one of the items from your list and determine not to spend that time on yourself. Instead, make it your priority this week to invest that time with God. Do this with another item from your list the following week until you are spending more of your available time on the things of God.

2. Think of the many things a parent does for his or her children. How many of those things has God done for you? How many things has He done that far exceed even those? What does that tell you about God's special love for you as His child? How does this relate to your anxiety? Take this time to thank God for His love and care for you. Then begin to turn your anxiety over to Him by committing to His care one of the things from your list in question 1.

## FOCUS ON PRAYER

To better internalize the priorities of your life, memorize 1 Corinthians 10:31: "Whether ... you eat or drink or whatever you do, do all to the glory of God." Meditate on that verse before the Lord and as you do, examine your heart attitude. Do you desire to give God glory because you love Him? Are you willing to be content and not worry—even if you have long tended to be a worrier—as one way of giving Him glory?

## ASSIGNMENT

Look up Genesis 3:18–19 and 2 Thessalonians 3:10. How has God designed for man to earn his food? What happens if he doesn't follow God's design? God will provide for man just like He does for the birds if man will only follow His design. Look up the following verses: Leviticus 26:3–5; Deuteronomy 5:32–33; 8:1; Jeremiah 38:20; John 12:26. What does God do for those who are obedient to Him? How do those verses relate to your worry over necessities? Instead of worrying, what should you be doing? Make it a point to seek God's kingdom and His righteousness by being obedient.

## CHAPTER 2
### AVOIDING ANXIETY THROUGH PRAYER

### CHAPTER THEME

From Philippians 4:6–9 we learn that the foremost way to avoid anxiety is through prayer. Right thinking and action are the next logical steps.

### ICEBREAKERS

1. When Jonah was swallowed by a great fish, he responded to his situation with thankful prayer. Speculate on how you would respond if you suddenly found yourself in Jonah's predicament. What do you think you'd say to God?

2. A friend confides to you that she is feeling at her wits' end because of her troubles. She wonders out loud if it's because she thinks too much about it all. Give a wise

response to her based on what you've
learned from Matthew 6 and Philippians 4.

## GROUP DISCOVERY QUESTIONS

1. What is the foremost way to avoid anxiety? Support your answer with Scripture.
2. How are we to pray?
3. Fill in the blanks: The real challenge of Christian living is not to eliminate every uncomfortable circumstance from our lives, but to _____ _____ in the midst of every situation.
4. When will the Lord give us His peace?
5. As we leave the sin of worry behind with our prayers, what is the next step in Christian maturity?
6. Fill in the blank: Faith is a _____ to revealed truth.
7. What is God's chief agent for purifying our thinking? Recite verses that support your answer.
8. Summarize the main things God's Word says we're to think about. How does that apply to anxiety?
9. What is the point of godly thinking?
10. How do godly attitudes, thoughts, and actions work together?
11. Fill in the blanks: Pure behavior produces spiritual _____ and _____.
12. What is the best protection from worry?

## PERSONAL APPLICATION QUESTIONS

1. Being anxious for nothing means trusting God completely in every circumstance we encounter. He can help us handle our problems, even when we don't understand them. When you face a new problem, are you more apt to pray about it or worry about it? Here are some of the most common problems Christians encounter. Match each one with the appropriate verse, and memorize those which speak to your needs:

   1. Financial difficulty          a. Romans 8:29–39
   2. Injustice                     b. Matthew 28:20
   3. Doubting your salvation       c. 1 John 1:9
   4. Feeling unforgiven by God     d. Psalm 37:1–11
   5. Loneliness                    e. Philippians 4:19

2. Do you experience the joy of answered prayer? One of the best ways to guarantee that you will is to keep a record of your prayer requests. As time goes along and you see prayers answered, you'll also clearly see God at work in your life. To make your own prayer log, write down your daily prayer requests and the date you make them. Then whenever a specific request is answered, put a check mark by it. Not only will this make you more aware of God's answers to your prayers, but it will also serve as a constant reminder of what God has done for you in the past.

That can be a great source of comfort
when the future looks uncertain.

## FOCUS ON PRAYER

The Puritan John Owen gave this analogy to show the
importance of continually focusing on spiritual things:

> The thoughts of spiritual things are with many,
> as guests that come into an inn, and not like
> children that dwell in the house. They enter
> occasionally, and then there is a great stir about
> them, to provide [suitable] entertainment for
> them. In a while they are disposed of, and so
> depart, being neither looked nor inquired after
> anymore. Things of another nature are attended
> to; new occasions bring in new guests, for a
> season.
>
> [However, children that dwell in the house]
> are missed if they are out of the way, and have
> their daily provision constantly made for them. So
> it is with these occasional thoughts about spiritual
> things. By one means or other they enter into the
> mind, and there are entertained for a season. On a
> sudden they depart, and men hear of them no
> more. But those that are natural and genuine, aris-
> ing from a living spring of grace in the heart,
> disposing the mind unto them, are as the children
> of the house; they are expected in their places, and
> at their seasons. If they are missing, they are
> inquired after. The heart calls itself to an account,
> whence it is that it hath been so long without
> them, and calls them over [for a desired conversa-
> tion] with them.[1]

With that in mind, make this your prayer: "Let the words of my mouth and the meditation of my heart be acceptable in Thy sight, O LORD, my rock and my redeemer" (Ps. 19:14).

## ASSIGNMENT

In his book *Spiritual Intimacy* Richard Mayhue wrote,

> To hear something once for most of us is not enough. To briefly ponder something profound … does not allow enough time to grasp and fully understand its significance. This proves to be most true with God's mind in Scripture. The idea of meditating sometimes lends itself to misunderstanding, so let me illustrate its meaning….
>
> For me, the most vivid picture comes from a coffee percolator. The water goes up a small tube and drains down through the coffee grounds. After enough cycles, the flavor of the coffee beans has been transferred to the water which we then call coffee. So it is that we need to cycle our thoughts through the "grounds" of God's Word until we start to think like God.[2]

Renew your mind by regularly meditating on God's Word. Doing so will bring into your mind what is spiritually healthy and lead you away from what is harmful, including anxiety. Try different Bibles and schedules designed to help you read through the entire Bible in a year's time. A chronological schema is especially helpful for getting you into the flow of God's Word as He revealed it in human history.

## CHAPTER 3
## CASTING YOUR CARES ON GOD

### CHAPTER THEME

First Peter 5:5–7 teaches that a humble attitude of trust in God and His timing enables us to truly hand over all our cares to Him.

### ICEBREAKERS

1. In John 13 Jesus gave a great illustration of humility by washing His disciples' feet. What are comparable illustrations relevant to our own culture that you have observed?
2. Suppose you are talking with a family member who resents what God's mighty hand has brought into his life. He seethes with resentment similar to that expressed by Omar Khayyám and Job. What could you say to him that might help?

### GROUP DISCOVERY QUESTIONS

1. From what comes the ability to truly hand over all your cares to God?
2. How did the ancient world view humility? How does that relate to modern times?

3. What is the practical application of the footwashing incident in John 13?

4. Fill in the blanks: From Jesus we learn that the first step to enjoying the blessings of humility is to stoop to serve even _____ _____.

5. What plain fact of spiritual life motivates us to be humble?

6. When faced with the awesomeness of God's omnipotence, what is a balancing factor to keep in mind?

7. Fill in the blanks: Never view the mighty hand of God in your life as a _____ _____ _____ _____ _____, but as _____ _____ _____.

8. Discuss God's timing in relation to present trials.

9. What does God want you to do with all your anxiety? Give an Old Testament example of someone who did that.

10. When you are bearing a great burden and someone treats you insensitively, thus making your burden heavier, what is a biblical way to respond?

11. What practical advice does Jay Adams give about stopping worry?

## PERSONAL APPLICATION QUESTIONS

1. How humble does the person closest to you think you are? One way to get an accurate answer is to ask that person what John 13 type of actions he or she

would most like to be the recipient of. After hearing the answer, think carefully: Have you done any of those things for that person?

2. Often we regard stress and suffering as if they're to be avoided at all costs. Robert Murray McCheyne reflected God's point of view when he wrote, "There is a great want about all Christians who have not suffered. Some flowers must be broken or bruised before they emit any fragrance."[3] Do you view whatever tends to make you anxious as something to be avoided or as an opportunity to project the fragrance of a transformed life?

## FOCUS ON PRAYER

We are prone to be more troubled about a great affliction we must suffer than about "trivial" sins like worry. Yet in God's way of looking at things, "There is more evil in a drop of sin than in a sea of affliction."[4] Ask the Lord to help you be more concerned about avoiding sin than about your personal comfort.

## ASSIGNMENT

Proverbs 15:33 says, "Before honor comes humility." How often do you get the order of the two mixed up? Read James 4:1–10. What happens when you exalt yourself? What happens when you humble yourself before God? Remember, "friendship with the world is hostility toward God" (v. 4). In this past week, have you shown any hostility toward God? Our world is characterized by pride—it is pervasive and defiling. Make it your goal this week to begin rooting out pride in your life by developing a more humble attitude.

## CHAPTER 4
## LIVING A LIFE OF FAITH AND TRUST

### CHAPTER THEME

The beginning of faith is the end of anxiety and vice versa. Hebrews 11—12 and the Psalms illustrate that in many ways.

### ICEBREAKERS

1. Pretend you are George Müller living in today's world. What is something tragic you see going on that you'd like to have the faith to help change for the better?
2. You are talking with a believer who is worried about how bad things are in our country. Keeping in mind what the servant of Bulstrode Whitelock said to his employer, how would you begin comforting and perhaps challenging this person?

### GROUP DISCOVERY QUESTIONS

1. How does faith relate to anxiety?
2. What are some things that weigh us down in the Christian life?
3. Fill in the blanks: Our actions reveal what we _____ _____.

4. How does the shield of faith work?

5. Fill in the blanks: In the Christian life, your focal point must be _____ _____. Explain what that means in relation to yourself and other Christians.

6. What awaits us at the finish line of the race of faith? Do we experience any of that in the here and now? Explain your answer.

7. When you start thinking it's too tough to live the Christian life nowadays, what should you consider?

8. How do humility and thankful prayer join together?

9. Fill in the blank: Anxiety cannot survive in an environment of _____.

10. What is God's hymnbook of praise?

11. What two things does true praise involve? Give an Old Testament example of someone who illustrates both.

## PERSONAL APPLICATION QUESTIONS

1. Do you possess little faith or large faith? Are the circumstances in your life determining how you behave rather than the Word of God? Do you know God well? If not, it's time to get to know Him better. Read Joshua 1:8. What does God promise to do for whomever will meditate on His Word day and night? Will you covenant with God to spend time in His Word daily?

2. Read Hebrews 11 and the Old Testament counterparts listed as cross-references. You will discover that faith demands risk. What risks did the Old Testament saints take because they knew that God is faithful in His promises? In spite of the temporary hazards you encounter, are you trusting God for things that will stretch your faith?

## FOCUS ON PRAYER

When life is difficult and your future seems unsure, how do you react? Does your Christian faith affect your view of life? Do you tend to place every trial, every thought regarding the future, and every present situation in the context of your faith? If not, you need to make some changes in your life. Begin those changes with prayer. As an incentive to your prayer, memorize James 5:16: "The prayer of a righteous man is powerful and effective" (NIV).

## ASSIGNMENTS

1. List as many of God's attributes as you can think of, and then list His gracious works in your life. Now make a list of the situations you tend to worry about. Recite God's attributes and works out loud in prayer, thanking Him for each one, and then look back at your list of problems. Like Habakkuk, you will find your anxiety fading.

2. Read the introduction to "Psalms for the
   Anxious" (this book's appendix).
   Schedule times over the course of a
   month or a year to follow through with
   the suggestions it gives.

# CHAPTER 5
## KNOWING OTHERS ARE LOOKING OUT FOR YOU

### CHAPTER THEME

As important as it is to engage in a personal war against
anxiety, God provides the ministry of angels and fellow
believers to aid you in your struggle.

### ICEBREAKERS

1. You are talking with a Christian mother
   whose biggest worry is her children. She
   admits to you that she can't stop fearing
   that something terrible might happen to
   them when they are out of her sight.
   How might you minister to her?
2. A good Christian friend is telling you
   about his sweet times of fellowship with
   the Lord. As the conversation progresses,
   however, it becomes clear that he is not
   involved regularly at any church, Bible
   study, or other type of Christian fellowship. His attitude could be summarized
   as "Just me and Jesus." How would
   Jesus have you respond to him?

## GROUP DISCOVERY QUESTIONS

1. How does Hebrews 1:14 describe angels?
2. What is one of God's main ways of making His children physically secure?
3. What reason did Billy Graham give for believing in angels?
4. Contrast the ways that the Holy Spirit and angels guide believers.
5. Give an Old Testament example of the providing or sustaining ministry of angels.
6. Contrast an angel's ability with a human's ability to protect someone.
7. Fill in the blanks: You can't ever get yourself into a situation that God _____ _____ _____ _____.
8. Explain how angels respond to our prayers.
9. What is a godly attitude to have toward angels?
10. Is it impossible to serve one another in the church with the same diligence as the angels serve us? Why or why not?
11. List the temporary spiritual gifts, then the permanent ones. Which of the permanent gifts are especially helpful for the church to deal with anxiety in its midst?
12. Mention some of the "one anothers" of the New Testament as related to the ministry of spiritual gifts.
13. According to Bruce Larson, why are bars so popular?

14. Name some of the things Christians don't do in true fellowship.
15. Describe the tragedy of the bubble Christian. What is the remedy?
16. Fill in the blanks: Never underestimate the power of _____ _____ in bearing the burden of your anxieties.

## PERSONAL APPLICATION QUESTIONS

1. Many in the church prayed fervently for God to release Peter when he was in prison (Acts 12:5). But when he was miraculously rescued by an angel, many of those who prayed for something like that to happen didn't believe it when it actually did take place (vv. 15–16). Are you praying for something you don't really expect God to come through on? Are you merely going through the motions of prayer? Be faithful in your prayers, and don't be surprised when God answers them. Read what Jesus said about the miraculous power of prayer in Mark 11:23–24; Luke 11:5–10; 18:1–8; and John 15:7.

2. Like Elijah, other faithful servants of God have become shortsighted and filled with despair. When our faith in God's power is gone, we lose our confidence and run from that which really shouldn't intimidate us. Opposition can paralyze us with fear and prevent us

from proclaiming God's truth. Read
Matthew 10:24–33. What did Jesus tell
His disciples? If you have an antagonistic
coworker, neighbor, or relative, pray
that God will give you boldness to speak
the truth in love.

## FOCUS ON PRAYER

Review Paul's experience on the high seas. After many
days of being at the storm's mercy, "all hope ... was then
taken away" (Acts 27:20 KJV). Sometimes God has to bring
people to their darkest point before they will look to Him.
There may be people around you who have lost all hope in
their work, marriage, or children. Their anxieties and disap-
pointments are bringing them to the breaking point. Pray for
sensitivity to their needs and that God might use you to offer
them words of hope from Scripture.

## ASSIGNMENTS

1. It's easy for us to take for granted God's
   many provisions for our physical and
   spiritual welfare. Read Psalms 34 and 91.
   Thank God for His unbounded grace
   and faithfulness. Thank Him for His
   angelic host, which works on our behalf
   in carrying out His perfect will.
2. Do your own in-depth study on angels
   by examining Hebrews 1—2. Divide a
   piece of paper in half and list the qualities
   attributed to the Son of God on one
   side and the corresponding qualities of

angels on the other. As you analyze chapter 1, consider Christ's relationship to the angels. In chapter 2, consider why Christ was made lower than the angels for a time.

3. List the different ways you have served your church on a regular basis. How many of those things are you still doing? Next to the things you aren't doing any-more, note how long you served in that capacity. Do you have a pattern of being involved in things for only a short period of time? For each of the things you aren't doing anymore, ask yourself why you stopped. Do you find your involve-ment may have been based on superficial things such as an emotional appeal or a temporary interest? Ask God for His guidance in your current areas of service, and make sure you have a true, enduring commitment to use your gifts to serve His church for life.

## CHAPTER 6
### DEALING WITH PROBLEM PEOPLE

### CHAPTER THEME

An effective way to attack anxiety in the church is to understand and minister to the problem groups in the church that Paul talked about in 1 Thessalonians 5:14–15.

## ICEBREAKER

You feel sorry for someone at church or Bible study who perpetually seems fearful, worried, melancholy, and depressed. What could you do for that person? What might you recommend that person do for himself or herself?

## GROUP DISCOVERY QUESTIONS

1. What is one of the ways the church grows spiritually?
2. Give a summary description of the five problem groups Paul mentioned.
3. What happens when you help a worrier not to worry?
4. How are we to deal with the wayward? Explain how to do that.
5. What is the solution to anxiety?
6. Why are people who are anxious usually depressed?
7. What specifically helps the worried to participate in the adventure of life?
8. Fill in the blanks: The church grows when the _____ help take care of the _____.
9. How would the Lord have us respond to the wearisome?
10. What is one of the most difficult circumstances we face in church life? How are we to respond to it?
11. What is the bigger picture on attacking anxiety?

## Personal Application Questions

1. Read Ephesians 5:27. How does Jesus Christ want to present the church to God? What responsibility does each church member have, then? What are you doing to help the church in that regard? How does your own life measure up? Are there any areas of your life that are married to the world? Name them. Confess them to God and repent of them. Make the commitment to keep your life unspotted by the world.

2. What are your plans for ministering to others in the next month? In the next year? In five years? In ten years? You may not be on the church staff, but you should still have a vision for the church's future. Do you recognize any needs you are prepared to meet now? Is the Lord bringing to your attention any needs you should start preparing yourself to meet? Prayerfully plan how you will accomplish those goals, even if they seem beyond your ability right now.

## Focus on Prayer

From Philippians 4:2–3 we learn that a personal disagreement between two women spread discord in the Philippian church. Jonathan Edwards made this observation:

When we suffer injuries from others, the case is often such that a Christian spirit, if we did but exercise it as we ought, would dispose us to forbear taking the advantage we may have to vindicate and right ourselves. For by doing otherwise, we may be the means of bringing very great calamity on him that has injured us; and tenderness toward him may and ought to dispose us to a great deal of forbearance, and to suffer somewhat ourselves, rather than bring so much suffering on him. And besides, such a course would probably lead to a violation of peace and to an established hostility, whereas in this way there may be hope of gaining our neighbour, and from an enemy making him a friend.[5]

Pray for the Lord to use you to cultivate harmony between believers through your love for them in word and deed.

## ASSIGNMENTS

1. If you are not already discipling someone, try to identify a Christian in your sphere of influence who could benefit from your spiritual maturity. Are you willing to share your life with that person as you help him or her to solve problems biblically? Since learning takes place best when there's a need to know, you will need to be available in crisis situations. Discipling someone isn't easy, but the joy

and sense of accomplishment it brings are more than worth the effort.

2. Read 1 Thessalonians. Evaluate yourself and the spiritual health of your church on the basis of seven characteristics you will find there:

- Are you and the majority of your church genuine as opposed to nominal Christians?
- Are you and they committed to being like Christ and willing to suffer for His sake?
- Are you and they regularly praying for opportunities to share the gospel? Does your church have a ministry for training people to evangelize?
- Are you and they living the kind of life that will lend credence to your message?
- Are you and they eagerly awaiting the return of Christ?
- Do you and they have a proper balance between love and sound doctrine?
- Are you and they supportive of church leaders or indifferent to what they are trying to accomplish?

If any of these elements are lacking in your life or in your church, determine what steps you can take to help strengthen those areas.

## CHAPTER 7
## HAVING PEACE IN EVERY CIRCUMSTANCE

### CHAPTER THEME

One of the lessons from 2 Thessalonians 3:16, 18 is that as we are what we ought to be, God infuses us with His peace and grace, and that has a wonderful way of crowding out anxiety.

### ICEBREAKER

Reflect on emergency situations you have been through in the past. Focus on one that is still clear in your mind. What do you remember thinking about at the time? What helped get you through the ordeal?

### GROUP DISCOVERY QUESTIONS

1. What is a common definition of peace? How does it fall short in explaining godly peace?
2. Fill in the blanks: The peace that God gives is not subject to the _____ of _____.
3. Describe peace as an attribute of God.
4. Cite Psalm 85:8. What is a New Testament parallel to that verse?
5. Summarize what Thomas Watson said about the false peace of the wicked.
6. How can the peace God gives His children be interrupted? How can it be restored?

7. What is one way of demonstrating to the world that Jesus keeps His promises?

8. How did God's grace help Paul in a trial that brought him great anxiety?

9. What are some of the things God's grace does for us? What are the conditions for receiving it?

## PERSONAL APPLICATION QUESTIONS

1. On the ocean's surface there is often great agitation, but underneath, the water becomes increasingly calm to the point of being virtually still. Survey teams dredging this calm area of the ocean floor have found animal and plant remains that appear to have been undisturbed for hundreds of years. This "cushion of the sea," as it is called by oceanographers, is like the peace experienced by Christians. Regardless of the anxiety and trouble in a Christian's surroundings, there is a cushion of peace in his soul. That's because he knows the Prince of Peace and has within him the Spirit of peace given by the God of peace. How is that area in your life? Are you allowing the turbulence around you to get down deep within you and disturb it?

2. It is easy to forget that peace with God inevitably results in war with the world. Vance Havner said,

Let it not be forgotten that a twice-born and Spirit-filled Christian is always a contradiction to this old world. He crosses it at every point. From the day that he is born again, until he passes on to be with the Lord he pulls against the current of a world forever going the other way.

If he allows it, men will tone him down, steal the joy of his salvation, reduce him to the dreary level of the average.... Most church folk dislike having their Laodicean complacency upset by those who insist on walking by faith and not by sight.[6]

Are you at peace with God or the world? A faith that draws peace from heaven finds life on earth a continual struggle. But it is the good fight of faith (1 Tim. 1:18–19).

## FOCUS ON PRAYER

In John 16:26 we learn that we have direct access to the Father through prayer. From Romans 8:26, 34 we learn that Christ will intercede for us when we need His help. What do those truths tell you about how much God wants to communicate with you and help you? Are you as passionate to pray to God as He is to listen to your prayers? Pray to Him about what's on your heart right now. His peace awaits you.

## ASSIGNMENT

Philippians 4:9 connects godly living with God's peace. Read Proverbs 1:33 and 28:1 to see that connection as well. Then write Philippians 4:6–9 on a card and memorize it. Ask for the Lord's help in overcoming anxiety when you are tempted to worry, meditating on the memorized Scripture. Doing so will reinforce godly thinking and living.

## CHAPTER 8
## DOING ALL THINGS WITHOUT COMPLAINING

### CHAPTER THEME

An important application of Philippians 2:14–16 is to avoid complaining.

### ICEBREAKERS

1. You are visiting with close Christian friends who have one young child. They love their child very much and are eager to cater to his wishes but are afraid of spoiling him. They ask your opinion on child raising. What would you say?

2. A family member has slipped into the bad habit of complaining about almost everything. It is driving you to distraction, and you find you don't even want to be around this person anymore. You value the relationship highly, however, and don't want it to disintegrate any further. How would you handle the situation?

## GROUP DISCOVERY QUESTIONS

1. What tendency comes with gaining wealth?
2. Why are small families in a materialistic society apt to produce discontented children?
3. What happens in most large families mainly because of logistics?
4. What is an unfortunate product of child-centered parenting?
5. What is one of the positive benefits for a child who conforms to authority?
6. Why don't many young people want to leave home? What kind of employees do they tend to be?
7. When materialistic individuals feel empty inside, what are they apt to do? How does that affect society at large?
8. What are some of the most common things people complain about?
9. When are our concerns productive?
10. Prove from Scripture that it is a sin to complain against God. Use Old and New Testament examples.
11. What is the only proper way to say thank you to God for forgiving our sins?
12. What does the Bible say about contentment, and where does it say it?
13. Why does God hate complaining so much?
14. What are two aspects of shining as lights in a dark world?
15. How does a complaining spirit affect others and the one who possesses it?

## PERSONAL APPLICATION QUESTIONS

1.  Are you presently lacking joy and con-
    tentment in your life? Here is a
    scriptural checklist for you to consider:
    • Are you obeying God's clearly
    revealed will as recorded in the Bible?
    (Ps. 119:111)
    • Are you aware of any unconfessed sin
    in your life? (Ps. 51:9, 12)
    • Are you sharing your faith with others
    and helping them to grow spiritually?
    (Phil. 2:17)
    • Are you filled with the Spirit, con-
    sciously yielding yourself to His
    control? (Gal. 5:19–26)
    • Are you characterized by a deep love
    for Christ? (1 Peter 1:8)

2.  Do you have the attitude that the Lord
    owns everything you have? Do you reg-
    ularly make a distinction between your
    needs and your wants? Do you avoid
    buying what you do not need and can-
    not use? Do you spend less than you
    make? Do you give sacrificially to the
    Lord's work? Being able to give an hon-
    est and wholehearted yes to all these
    questions is crucial to being content
    with what you have and free from the
    love of money (cf. 1 Tim. 6:6–10).

## FOCUS ON PRAYER

The Israelites enjoyed tremendous spiritual privileges, as 1 Corinthians 10 attests. List the benefits you enjoy because of your relationship with Christ. Take time each day this week to meditate on those benefits and praise God for His matchless grace in giving them to you—especially when you find yourself tempted to complain about something.

## ASSIGNMENT

Make a general list of what you own, with your name on top. When you finish, cross out your name and write "God's" in its place. Then specifically thank God for everything on that list. From now on, carefully plan your trips to the store. The only things that should be on your list are what you actually need and can afford. Don't get caught in the trap of spending more than you make. Finally, determine what you can afford to give to the Lord's work and then try to give a little more than that. You will be making a sacrifice that will reap eternal rewards.

## CHAPTER 9
## LEARNING TO BE CONTENT

## CHAPTER THEME

In Philippians 4:10–19 Paul is a model of being confident of God's providence, satisfied with little, not distressed by one's circumstances, sustained by divine power, and preoccupied with the well-being of others.

## ICEBREAKERS

1. A ministry you have respected is starting to resort to panic and manipulation to gain support. How might you use Philippians 4 to concisely and precisely express your concern to the ministry's directors?

2. Your child tells you he or she needs a new toy. Your spouse tells you he or she needs a new hobby. Help them figure out what they really need by helping them think through their use of the word *need*. How could you do that in a tactful way?

## GROUP DISCOVERY QUESTIONS

1. Fill in the blank: The Bible speaks of contentment not only as a virtue but also as a _____.

2. What was Paul's situation when he was writing the book of Philippians?

3. Explain the Stoic view of contentment. How does the biblical concept differ?

4. Describe the course of Paul's relationship with the church at Philippi and its relevance to the closing of his letter to them.

5. What was Paul confident of in God's ordering the circumstances of his life?

6. What are the two ways God acts in the world? Compare them with one another.

7. How can you keep your confidence in the providence of God from declining into a fatalistic attitude?

8. What's one way to protect yourself from our materialistic culture's redefinition of human needs?

9. How can we as Christians lose our sense of satisfaction and peace? How can we get them back?

10. What increases our capacity to experience contentment? Give one important qualifier.

11. Why don't many of us experience contentment? Give some examples.

12. What was Paul more interested in than his material gain?

13. What is a good Scripture verse to use as a spiritual lifeline in attacking anxiety?

## PERSONAL APPLICATION QUESTIONS

Are you encountering any difficult circumstances in your life right now? In light of Romans 8:28, what perspective should you have regarding your situation? Does that perspective apply to every situation you might encounter? As a Christian you have every reason to be optimistic. Don't allow adversity to obscure God's promise that all things will ultimately work out for your good.

## FOCUS ON PRAYER

What kind of example does Paul provide for us in Philippians 4? Why was he content? What were the "all things" he could do through Christ? According to verse 19, what happens to those who risk their future well-being by sharing their possessions to meet a need? What needs are you aware of that exist presently in the body of Christ? Do you have the resources to meet one of those needs? If so, is there anything that should prevent you from meeting that need? Ask God to give you the wisdom to best employ the resources He has given you to meet that need. Then thank Him for the privilege.

## ASSIGNMENT

It is so easy for us to be preoccupied with the problems and issues of the moment and forget about the wondrous joys that await us in eternity. Take a few minutes now to meditate on Revelation 21:1–22:5. What are some things to look forward to in your *new home?* How will life be different from what it is now? Frequently thinking about your future home will give you an eternal and refreshing perspective that results in giving thanks and praise to God.

# SCRIPTURE INDEX

# SUBJECT INDEX

# NOTES

## Introduction

1. Marian V. Liautaud, *Today's Christian Woman,* July/August 1991, 24.
2. John MacArthur, Jr., *Our Sufficiency in Christ* (Dallas: Word, 1991).
3. Glenna Whitley, "The Seduction of Gloria Grady," *D Magazine,* October 1991, 45–71.
4. Ibid., 69.
5. Ibid., 71.
6. Frank, Minirth, Paul Meier, and Don Hawkins, *Worry-Free Living* (Nashville: Thomas Nelson, 1989), 113–14.

## Chapter 1

1. Sir Arthur Conan Doyle, *The Complete Sherlock Holmes* (New York: Doubleday, 1927).
2. United States Department of Agriculture, *Is the World Facing Starvation?,* Office of Governmental and Public Affairs, June 1979, 4.

3. Ibid., 5.
4. Jay Adams, *What Do You Do When You Worry All the Time?* (Phillipsburg, NJ: P&R Publishing Company, 1975).
5. Ibid.
6. Anton Chekhov, *The Bet and Other Stories* (Dublin and London: Maunsel & Company, 1915), 9–11.

## CHAPTER 2

1. Paul S. Rees, *The Adequate Man: Paul in Philippians* (Westwood, NJ: Revell, 1959), 106.
2. D. Martyn Lloyd-Jones, *The Sermon on the Mount* vol. 2 (Grand Rapids, MI: Eerdmans, 1960), 129–30.
3. Jay Adams, *What Do You Do When Fear Overcomes You?* (Phillipsburg, NJ: P&R Publishing Company, 1975).

## CHAPTER 3

1. John MacArthur, Jr., *How to Meet the Enemy* (Wheaton, IL: Victor, 1992).
2. Jay Adams, *What Do You Do When Fear Overcomes You?* (Phillipsburg, NJ: P&R Publishing Company, 1975).
3. Thomas à Kempis, *The Imitation of Christ,* Translated by Geoffrey Cumberlege (New York: Oxford University Press, n.d.).

## CHAPTER 4

1. Arthur T. Pierson, *George Müller of Bristol* (Grand Rapids, MI: Fleming H. Revell, 1899), 437.
2. Walter B. Knight, *Three Thousand Illustrations for Christian Service* (Grand Rapids, MI: Eerdmans, 1947), 740.

## Chapter 5

1. C. S. Lewis, *The Lion, the Witch and the Wardrobe* (New York: Macmillan, 1970), 125.
2. Billy Graham, *Angels: God's Secret Agents* (New York: Doubleday, 1975), 115.
3. John MacArthur, Jr., *Charismatic Chaos* (Grand Rapids, MI: Zondervan, 1992).
4. Bruce Larson, *Dare to Live Now!* (Grand Rapids, MI: Zondervan, 1965), 110.
5. Dietrich Bonhoeffer, *Life Together* (New York: Harper & Row, 1954), 112.

## Chapter 7

1. John MacArthur, Jr., *God: Coming Face to Face with His Majesty* (Wheaton, IL: Victor, 1993).
2. Thomas Watson, *A Body of Divinity* (Carlisle, PA: The Banner of Truth Trust, 1986), 262.

## Chapter 8

1. Chuck Colson and Jack Eckerd, *Why America Doesn't Work* (Dallas: Word, 1991).

## Chapter 9

1. William Barclay, *The Letters to the Philippians, Colossians, and Thessalonians* (Philadelphia: Westminster, 1959), 104.
2. T. R. Glover, *Progress in Religion to the Christian Era* (New York: George H. Doran, 1922), 233–39.

## Readers' Guide

1. John Owen, *The Grace and Duty of Being Spiritually Minded* (Grand Rapids, MI: Baker, 1977), 62–63.
2. Richard Mayhue, *Spiritual Intimacy* (Wheaton, IL: Victor, 1990), 46–47.
3. Robert Murray McCheyne, *More Gathered Gold: A Treasury of Quotations for Christians*, edited by John Blanchard (Welwyn, UK: Evangelical Press, 1986), 315.
4. Thomas Watson, *More Gathered Gold: A Treasury of Quotations for Christians*, edited by John Blanchard (Welwyn, UK: Evangelical Press, 1986), 325.
5. Jonathan Edwards, *Charity and Its Fruits*, edited by Tryon Edwards (Edinburgh: The Banner of Truth Trust, 1986), 74.
6. Vance Havner, *The Secret of Christian Joy* (New York: Revell, 1938), 54–55.